144,000 Points of Light:

The Resurrection of the Legions of Archangel Michael

By Alana Kay

*144,000 Points of Light: The Resurrection
of the Legions of Archangel Michael*

By Alana Kay
www.alanakay.com

Copyright 2016
ISBN: 978-0-9727232-2-0

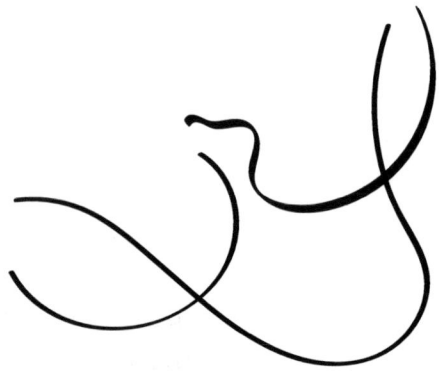

VIOLET PHOENIX PUBLISHING

Maui, Hawaii 96753

All quotes from A Course in Miracles are from the Second Edition, 1996, ©Foundation for Inner Peace, P.O. Box 598, Mill Valley, 94942-0598, www.acim.org and info@acim.org.

All rights reserved. No part of this book may be used or reproduced by any means, graphic, electronic, or mechanical, including photocopying, recording, taping or by any information storage retrieval system without the written permission of the publisher except in the case of brief quotations embodied in critical articles and reviews.

Table of Contents

Preface

Golden Angels & Fallen Angels 11

Holier Than Thou: Keeping Spiritual Ego in Check 19

Christ Jesus, the Church and the Holy Bible 25

Spiritually Correct: Doing Away With One-Size-Fits-All Spirituality 31

Karma From the Viewpoint of Akasha 41

Act Your Soul Age: Energy Integrity For Old Souls 53

Crystal Clear: Energetic Freedom 63

Christ Consciousness Through the Twelve Aspects of Spiritual Love 69

Bonus Material: Meditation Made Simple 103

About the Author 109

"We are stardust
Billion-year-old carbon
We are golden
Caught in the devil's bargain
And we've got to get ourselves
Back to the garden"

-Joni Mitchell

Preface

The Legions of Archangel Michael are the oldest soul family in embodiment on Earth at this time and they are the 144,000 that have been referred to in esoteric teachings throughout time. You may be a member of this soul family or you may know one of them. The essence of Archangel Michael is the creative force of our planet and it is expressed through these souls. They are the spiritual elders. During this critical time of restoration of planet Earth, this soul group's presence is critical because the blueprint thereof lies in the electromagnetic data of their bodies.

How do you know if you are one of the 144,000? If you are reading this book, there is a good chance you are one of the 144,000. Furthermore, if that statement set off energy bursts within your being, it is ever more likely that you are one of this group and you have come to the right place. The bursts of energy are the sensation of the firing up of latent soul memories as they are being set free and sent forth. Only those who carry the blueprint of this soul group would feel the energizing impact of its mention. I have given you this energetic blast intentionally, so that you learn to recognize these kinds of things and to help awaken your soul.

Appearances have nothing to do with identification of members of this group. As a matter of fact, the lives of these souls are often very problematic.

Do you have an addictive personality, messy relationships and suicidal thoughts? Have you been diagnosed as bi-polar, have a central nervous system disease or an autoimmune disease? When you were young, did you feel like a stranger in a strange land? Have you always believed in Love and wondered why Love is not revered as it should be?

On the lighter side, have you experienced a very significant spiritual awakening or feel that you have always been in touch with your soul but not sure what to do? Are you so empathetic that you feel everybody's pain as well as their joy? Have you been accused of being a Pollyanna? Do you cry easily? Do you care deeply about the innocent, the animals and the environment? Do you have deep and amazing insights that you do not act on?

Although these traits are not exclusive to the 144,000, they are very common in this soul group and these manifestations are merely symptoms of those who have forgotten whom they are and why they are here. Symptoms such as these are just the tip of the iceberg, and could be a sign that you have come here to help lead humanity to the next step in their evolution – invoking a spiritual power that serves the purpose of enlightening and empowering others. The energy has to go somewhere and if it does not, it implodes on itself.

As Golden Angels, many of us chose to be incarnated into dysfunctional families or very difficult circumstances. For a few moments, try to sense what it may have been like to look at the world before embodiment. What appears obvious to us may not be so obvious to others – we needed to develop strong compassion for those we came to serve. Choosing challenging life circumstances didn't seem like too much of an undertaking, but upon arrival in the denser energies, we forgot our mission and purpose. We forgot who we truly are. We started to believe what we were being fed and essentially got lost in the chaos.

This duplicity created massive inner confusion; causing us to experience high highs and low lows, amazing days and horrible days. This is why I am trying to wake you up and ask you to believe only the really good stuff because that is the only thing that is real and eternal. The rest is human error. Forgive the human error both on the part of others and your self. We are here to become the embodiment of Christ Consciousness and the vehicle for change. We are not supposed to buy into this chaos and become victims of society.

Before I begin, I want to emphasize that the 144,000 are not members of a specific religious group. Nor are they spiritually superior to other beings. Their experience here on Earth is a double-edged sword. They are the spiritual elders and therefore have a high level of commitment and responsibility. They have stepped down from higher realms to bridge the higher frequencies with those on Earth. They are like the parents of all earth inhabitants and have incarnated en masse at this time to seed a higher level of consciousness on our arisen planet.

The Legions of Archangel Michael, whose programming is Christ Consciousness, are currently incarnated as any ethnic group or religion – wealthy or poor – healthy or chronically ill – female, male or other – young or old –

any variety of backgrounds or soul histories. At the same time, they are a soul group with a common purpose – to correct the course of humanity on planet Earth.

The world awaits the awakening of the spiritual leadership. Many are called, but few are chosen. Challenges must be overcome. As members of this soul group, we do this by becoming the embodiment of Love and becoming our authentic selves. It sounds easy, but it takes patience and persistence.

These turbulent times are ripe for the awakening of our soul group. It is time we understood our soul history and do the work necessary to reestablish our connection to divine consciousness. This manual should help you begin to understand these concepts and learn the special tools necessary to handle this delicate yet powerful equipment.

One of the primary reasons that I am writing this book is to debunk some of the info that has been written previously – much of which is loaded with religious jargon. This religious separation has caused many a solid spiritualist to turn away from their spiritual quest. Organized religion is often fraught with dark and oppressive, self-righteous, narrow-minded perspectives – a virtual dead end street.

On the contrary, Christ Consciousness is all encompassing and empowering and therefore fertile ground for spiritual growth. This is the seed we need to plant – firmly and eternally - Christ Consciousness is not moral judgment; it is unconditional Love and expansiveness. Organized religion does not corner the market on judgmental behavior; the spiritual new age has also lost its way by becoming too judgmental and too materially oriented.

The goal is Heaven on Earth.
The operating system is Love.

Why do we have to believe there is a plan? For one thing, it anchors us in a knowing that gives us great inner peace amid the turmoil. To put it simply, if you were to start a company, you would have a business plan and a mission statement. A computer has to have an operating system. Would planet Earth have been created with anything less? Search your soul and you will know that you have never doubted that there is a divine order to things here. Deep inside of you, there is recognition that there is a divine design to this place that is unfathomable to our human minds – yet you honor it and trust it. Look closely at a flower and you cannot help but know. You always have. It is part of who you are.

Yet, doubt creeps in. Our hearts keep at least a spark of gold, while our minds become entangled in this chaotic web that has come to occupy this sacred space. The mind begins to trick us out of believing what we know in our hearts to be true. Egos and differing viewpoints get in the way. A gold heart with a distorted ego creates what is known as spiritual ego. Ego is false personality and it may manifest as arrogance, withdrawal or illness. Members of this soul group are particularly vulnerable to this malady.

Still, the world awaits our awakening. We must release the Love and life that is in our hearts and regain our trust in its power. We need to drop the strong opinions and judgment that is born of spiritual ego, open our spiritual vision and ask our souls what we need to do to help bring this planet back into alignment with its original plan. We all came here with unique talents and passions and our purpose is written on our heart. Our soul actually pulsates electro magnetic data through our feeling center and all we really have to do is breathe our lives into existence. Psalm 40:8 from the Bible says, "I desire to do your will my God, your law is within my heart." Now imagine how hard it is on our bodies and minds to ignore this power and constantly push it down – refusing to let it be free. Withholding is very painful.

Folks may refuse to set their souls free on an individual level, but collectively, no matter what people do to distort Earth's destiny, it will always be corrected and re-routed – even if it has to kick humans off of it. Evil cannot sustain in this energy. It is at best short lived. This is one thing you must never forget. The darkness will and has tricked us out of believing this, but without our firm commitment to become Love and never, ever forget again, we will not accomplish our mission here at this time. Persist, and when you feel you cannot go on, keep practicing gentle breathing and persist longer. The darkness gives up in time. It is not as strong as the light.

This time around we are engulfed in the mission to beat all missions. Because the world is in such karmic chaos, many of the members of this soul group have opted out of their purpose and I would classify them as fallen angels. These fallen angels often become the ranks of homeless, mentally ill and substance abusers. Our worst enemy is our propensity to take responsibility for everything and to implode upon our selves in self-doubt and self-hatred.

This is another thing we must keep in balance.

No matter who you believe you are, in your core you are an Earth angel.

I have compassion for the fallen angels because I know it is not easy to be deep and sensitive while being incarnated on this planet at this time. We need to be forgiving, compassionate and helpful in really large doses – without damaging our own being and never giving up. We forgive and Love our self first and then turn that unconditional Love outward toward all of humanity. This is tricky business, but the darkest hour is just before the dawn.

The resurrection of humanity is going to require a great deal of creative problem solving and more miraculous healing than ever before. The "powers that be" at this time are either deceiving us or do not have the ability to lead with a heart that is connected to Source (God/Love). The Universe always fills a void. Let us fill the void of strong leadership with connected people whose purpose it is to lead.

The world needs the 144K to wake up and lead. We must open and heal our hearts first.

This group has the depth, the wisdom and the power to create Heaven on Earth – the divine plan and destiny of our planet. Stepping down to be of service can be very difficult and escapism is understandable. It is time to come out of the closet. We must bring ourselves into impeccable integrity – aligning mind, body and spirit with unconditional Love for our selves first. We must be still and learn once again to listen to the wisdom and accumulated knowledge of our souls. We must be living examples of what we believe and teach.

Create a life that is a living, breathing alter to spirit.

Because there are unique qualities inherent to the 144K, special tools are needed to revive and protect their energy. Even though I have lived many lifetimes before this one, the times we live in are particularly challenging. This guidebook has as much information as I could possibly gather after a lifetime of searching, discussing and experimenting. As with all of my writings and teachings, I do this out of Love and belief in humanity. I have often wanted to just go about living my life and let others to their own devices, knowing eventually everything will unfold, as it must. However, the information I have gathered nags at me day in and day out – wanting to find its way onto paper. I feel deep contentment when I write my books, so I do it. If there is something that nags you day in and day out, you need to start to do it and expect Spirit to help you. Let's be done with excuses. This is a priority.

While this high vibrational state is available to all beings, the Legions of Archangel Michael have carried this spark, however bright or dim from the time of their inception as an entity. Even when we are silent and simply enjoying life, we are laying energy pathways on Earth.

I have been a lifetime devotee to God with a greater opening and acceleration occurring when I was about 34 years old (1994). Most everything in this book comes from my personal experiences, synchronistic sharing with others or deep meditation, unless otherwise specified. I have asked the Ascended Masters to help me frequently throughout my life. Because I am able to remain in a high vibration most of the time, I am able to communicate with them readily. I can ask them anything and I will get an answer within 24 hours, if not immediately.

There is so much for all inhabitants of Earth to learn and the beings on this planet need to get up to speed with at least the bare minimum of spiritual understanding to feel comfortable in the new energy. There have been some fantastic books written in the last few decades that I believe are priceless. I have listed suggested reading at the end of each chapter. My suggestion as always is to be open to everything and discerning of everything. Accept only what resonates with your inner being and keep the other things in a mental file for future consideration.

Lastly, we are not waiting for somebody or something to save us. The heroes are you and I. This is the thought process we must engage in and teach others - impeccable, unbreakable self-responsibility. We are the world, we are the economy and we are the saviors. The government and the economy are merely a reflection of our communal energy and mentality. If you want to change the world, increase your capacity for Love. Become the change you want to see. Embrace and be your authentic self. Be Golden.

Suggested Reading:
A New Earth by Eckhart Tolle
Bringers of the Dawn by Barbara Marciniak

Golden Angels & Fallen Angels

Archangel Michael is a Golden Angel. As fragments of Archangel Michael, our soul vibrates in the very high frequency of gold, which manifests on the physical plane as deep violet. This is one reason that you will see depictions of Archangel Michael in the colors purple and gold. This is also one of the subconscious reasons we are so enamored with the precious metal gold.

As I have mentioned, this frequency comes with a high level of responsibility. It can cause us to feel high-highs and low-lows because it comes with a great deal of power and goes off balance easily. Balancing and focusing the power of Spirit is the highest of endeavors. We have been led to believe that building our retirement account and accumulating status and wealth are our greatest priorities. Balancing and using our power is the most important thing we can do at this time in the evolution of the planet and humanity. Once we do this, it becomes our anchor during chaos and uncertainty.

This energetic disposition causes us to be highly sensitive to everything. At the same time it has great attraction power for all things. Power, no matter what the source, has been used for great things and it has been used to manipulate and destroy. In its pure golden state, this power that comes from pure unconditional Love or Christ Consciousness creates, solves problems, brings forth genius and empowers all. This is called co-creation.

When cloaked in darkness, it can be very destructive, manipulative and self-serving. Unbeknownst to the abuser, it ends up imploding on the host. When it is not protected and directed by etheric forces, it absorbs negativity and becomes a cosmic battering ram. With great power caches at our disposal, we are merely energy stewards and we need to understand how to manage and focus this spiritual force.

At their core, Golden Angels are pure creative essence or Love. Some folks feel this is obvious and elementary, while many wonder what Love is. The spiritual Love that I speak of is unconditional Love and I go into this deeper, later on in this book. All esoteric teachings including the Bible attempt to explain Love. There are twelve aspects of unconditional Love that create the essence of the highest vibration available on Earth at this time. In sacred geometry, ether or higher consciousness is represented by the dodecahedron, which has twelve facets. These facets are Faith, Honesty, Generosity, Joy, Gentleness, Patience, Appreciation, Open-Mindedness, Expansiveness, Trust, Tolerance and Kindness. As spiritual leaders we must hold all of our lessons up to this light in order to validate our return to our soul and connection to higher consciousness. These ingredients are the fabric from which our souls are wrought.

When I think of famous people like Michael Jackson and Robin Williams I am reminded of the bi-polar nature of Golden Angels. These living examples had been at times both golden and fallen; fulfilling their purpose so wonderfully, yet suffering so deeply on a personal level. As with many others, drugs became a very destructive force in their lives. Other Golden Angels such as Paul McCartney and John Lennon connected and disconnected through time, but rebounded quite nicely. Many such as Stevie Ray Vaughn, Jim Croce, Ricky Nelson and Patsy Cline left us too soon because of their out of balance behavior. It does not matter who you are – if you are severely out of balance, you become subject to catastrophic errors. The more power you have, the greater the potential for imbalances.

One thing that happens to many a Golden Angel when they reach a certain level of fame or notoriety is they don't understand the power and advantage they have been given. Many have used it to build opulent homes and consume insane quantities of drugs. Some also become addicted to the thrill of being a star. Very few have understood that their charisma was destined to be a game changer in the world and that it was to be used for the benefit of humankind in some manner.

Anything that we have, energetically or physically is from Source/God and we are only stewards of that energy as we are stewards of this planet. Remember, we are all in this together and in the end, we are all one. What we do unto one, including ourselves, we do to the masses. The energy of God does not truly belong to anybody. We can't let the power get to our heads. It is the power that is in us, but not of us. Getting too full of ourselves takes us into egotistical behavior patterns.

All humans are of equal importance and value, but energy and experience differs from one human to another, depending on how the person is managing their energy. To begin with, we have very little of our cosmic energy in our bodies. Our entire causal body cannot fit in our earthly vessels. The more we use our energy for the benefit or advancement of humanity, the more of it that we are given. We also need to take very good care of our physical vessel – understanding and working with its biology and divine design – in order to be a strong and clear channel for spirit. This bestowing of energy follows us from lifetime to lifetime. Our soul is in charge of increasing our energy supply in our current embodiment, but our causal body can only be built upon by doing good works. This is one of the reasons why we feel a burst of energy or a resonance when we feel or speak something that is in line with the goals and knowledge of our soul.

When one uses energy for egotistical goals or negativity, energy levels begin to drop and motives can become self-destructive. The split mind believes it is still aligned with greatness, when in fact the deeds have become destructive. This is a very confusing state to be in. It's not that spirit is being mean or punishing those who misuse their power, this is simply how metaphysical laws operate. It is similar to cellular production or any form of increase. All true power comes from one Source/God/Love and when one disconnects from that Source, the energy dissipates or collapses. We did not create Love; Love created us. We simply have to understand and cooperate with the system. We cannot force it to do our will.

Deep, talented children who grow up in abusive, neglectful or oppressive environments can become criminals if there is no outside intervention. Conversely, I have seen young people respond to the slightest positivity and direction if they are blessed enough to encounter a mentor some where along the way. Many of the yet to be awakened spiritual leaders are destined to help guide these young geniuses. At the same time, there are many who overcome earlier difficulty without outside intervention and do magnificently well. It really depends on the individual.

So many of our institutions such as government, schools and work places are outdated and geared to creating a herd mentality. All of these institutions need to evolve in order to co-create a new world that supports individuality and reveres the beauty of life and spirit. However, the right people need to step up to the plate and transform and lead these institutions. We need leaders who are wise and who honor all life, not tyrannical leaders who believe that people should be under their control. Highly evolved leaders know how to do so with authority, respect and Love.

*Are you destined to be a leader on
our resurrected planet?*

We have not had leaders who are coming from a place of connection to spirit. The spiritual answers are often a blend of viewpoints with some highlights added. Disconnected individuals do not take all things in to consideration when deciding things and derive a lopsided view. We experience the dysfunction of polarization when we continually miss the mark. We have not known how to choose the right leadership either.

The dysfunctional leadership of our country is a reflection of our communal dysfunctional consciousness – it can be no other way. Nothing exists outside of our minds – everything is merely an out-picturing of consciousness. As a society, we have not truly embraced responsibility and service. The government will not save us or change us. We are the ones who need to save our selves and change. In the meantime, things are running amuck.

In the end all things in Heaven end up being used for the benefit of the light, because it is the divine blueprint and destiny of all things that are known and unknown. Survival of the fittest is not simply a scientific fact, it is a metaphysical fact – set forth to insure that the light always dominates. It can be no other way. Anybody or anything that tries to convince you otherwise is coming from fear and wanting to take you with them. Rest assured the light will win.

Fear is the big no-no these days. Fear will pull you into the chaos like a siphon. Fear will keep you trapped in the third dimension. Everything is always moving up even if it looks like it is taking a detour. The darkness knows how to create fear and keep us disconnected. Trust that everything always lands on its feet including humanity.

It is said that Lucifer, whose name means light bearer, descended into matter to transmute the darkness. This too, became an available band of consciousness and it served the purpose of highlighting the darkness or antimatter in order to return it to the violet field of creation. Also, I have found that some people play the role of darkness for the betterment of the whole. These people have the potential to teach us valuable karmic lessons. I am not alone in noticing that characters such as Adolf Hitler merely served as a vehicle to demonstrate the hatred and judgment that lay in all of our psyches. He became the outward manifestation of our communal patterns. His unimaginable behavior did in fact cause many a soul to approach human relationships differently and the positive, evolutionary effects of his horrible legacy still lingers.

Still others say that Lucifer had been given a reign of darkness by the karmic board and it is now over. I think this is most likely true but simply another way of describing a different perspective. There are some who believe that dark beings came out of the center of the Earth and got trapped in our realm, with no option but to attach to our energy because they had no eternal life source. Some say they came here from Mars just before their planet was destroyed by their misuse of power.

There are many different postulations about how darkness came to live here and I think it is wise to check in with your own soul memory and that of others in order to determine what you believe. Once we accept many perspectives and look at the deeper meaning, we often find the common thread. You will most likely find that all theories have the same happy ending. Most suggest the reign of evil on planet Earth is over. That is my humble belief and viewpoint as well.

Once again our salvation lies in the fact that the darkness is human error, whereas the light is eternal and of God. Both have existed in our physical and mental realities simultaneously. The most powerful statement in this regard resides in the opening phrase of *A Course in*

Miracles. "Nothing real can be threatened. Nothing unreal exists. Herein lies the peace of God." We only need correct the projection to see a different world.

Holier Than Thou: Keeping Spiritual Ego in Check

I talk a lot about spiritual empowerment because we live in a world that has a tendency to smash, quell and overshadow our spirits. On the other hand I believe that people with big spiritual egos are equally destructive.

Spiritual ego results from a false positioning of authority, value or importance based on a limited perspective. A person who has been studying spirituality for a long time or for many lifetimes, comes to understand that we all have a brilliant spirit and that we shouldn't judge because we are all on different positions of the ascension spiral. Newbies to spirituality or religion often become very preachy and judgmental. One should not consider his or her self enlightened unless they can see the brilliant spirit of others. Before one hangs out their shingle, I suggest they be capable of seeing what is right before they try to fix what is wrong. Ultimately, it is about all of us dreaming a different dream and creating a new paradigm, rather than fixing what is wrong with the old paradigm.

In order to dispense true healing energy or preach the gospel, one needs to be aligned with the highest vibration possible. If one does not have spiritual integrity and attempts to serve or heal, it is tantamount to someone trying to conduct surgery without going to medical school.

I am not trying to clip the wings of people who are in the process of climbing the spiritual ladder, I am simply encouraging people to be very careful about forming opinions of the world and of others until they have experienced the many, many facets of spiritual understanding, and even then I suggest we tread lightly. Spiritual knowledge is infinite, ever expanding and always building upon itself. It is understandable that when one has epiphanies they want to share with others. There never comes a time when we can say that we are in a position to judge or look down on others.

At the very least, I am suggesting that people who call themselves spiritual people shouldn't go around shaming, healing and disregarding others because they found a religion they like or have had a few insightful moments about the other side of life. There is not a group of saved or chosen people. There is no church or person who saves people. There is no singular book or person who has all the answers. Furthermore, all people and all books have their elements of truth even though some of what they espouse is faulty. Everything is in flux and for the most part, a mixed bag.

In the end, there are really only two choices. It is up to the individual to choose their spirit, which is what it means to be saved. Atonement is the term that is used in A Course in Miracles to describe one who has returned to their soul. One can only atone his or her self – with the help of God. At that point, a whole new world and perspective opens up. First we save or atone our own being and it is up to others to share in that journey. It is not ours to judge where they are on their journey, unless that is your job by grand design. It's an inside job. People will rise when they are ready.

While it is my life's mission to teach people about Love and Christ Consciousness, it is not my job to monitor the behavior and thoughts of others. I believe that we all have thoughts and feelings that are not of the highest vibration at times. It is challenging to try to keep the mouth shut and disengage the mind when one sees others "behaving badly." I believe that we are entitled to our opinions, right or wrong. All of this is part of our growth.

I don't believe we should be judging people so harshly (shaming) and attempting to be the thought police for everybody. This includes our families, neighbors, friends and even public figures. I am not talking about people who are causing damage to us, breaking the law or intentionally trying to deceive – these are most likely karmic issues that we need to address.

Some believe that judgmental behavior is more prominent in organized religion, but I find it to be rampant in many of the spiritual new agers and it is certainly rampant in pop culture. Facebook is replete with harsh, snappy judgment and pedestal hopping. I hear new agers talking about people's energy and calling it good or bad, and even condemning entire groups of people. In fact, many people who consider themselves spiritual can at times be the most egotistical; harshly judging the world through their own clogged filters.

We really need to think about how much time and energy we spend on the assessment of others. We need to begin to weigh this against the amount of energy we put into making the world a better place. If one considers his or her self to be a spiritual leader, there is certainly an area where they should be applying their good graces. I always say, "If you want to change the world, increase your capacity for Love." Dogging or shaming others to change has never been the answer.

If we are shutting out or trying to shut down any group or opinion because is does not meet our current expectations, then we are not as enlightened as we thought. Being enlightened requires us to be open minded and ever expanding. We should be able to allow others to process their own opinions. This is what is meant by the Law of Allowing as taught by Abraham (through Esther Hicks) and it is also referred to as tolerance in A Course in Miracles. Tolerance is an aspect of Love.

Be open to everything and at the same time, be discerning of everything. Have the strength to hear all sides of an issue and be willing to discover that you may not be 100% right in your original assumptions. Once again, I am not advocating the support of people who intentionally do serious damage to others.

Unconditional Love infuses everything with the energy of creation and therefore transforms everything. This is also known as transmutation. We need to stop demonizing people.

The solutions we seek in the future will come from the amalgamation of a variety of viewpoints. The reason we have such polarization is that everybody is a little wrong and everybody is a little right. Get ready to be open to others and not become judgmental.

As I said earlier, we do live in a world that has a strong tendency to be oppressive to the spirit. While I want to help others to see that their spirit is their power and how to restore and to use that power, we don't want to go overboard and take power and dominion over others. If one is that powerful, they should be leading others out of darkness by helping them become empowered also.

24   144,000 Points of Light

Christ Jesus, The Church & The Holy Bible

When it comes to getting to the core of many of humankind's issues, I believe that this trifecta causes the most arguments – effectively preventing sharing and brainstorming that would be so helpful to us now. I would like us to stop arguing about these things and get on with our lives. What I am going to be saying here is based on my personal experience, sharing with others, and my questions to the Ascended Masters as well as guidance from my inner voice. I am sure I won't quell all arguments about Jesus, church and the Bible, but I believe that maybe some open-minded discussion will bridge the gap for many.

To begin with, there are two groups of people who are like oil and water. These two groups are 1) those that believe that Jesus is Lord and savior and died for our sins and 2) those that believe that Jesus is a fictitious character. If people from these two groups were in the room with me right now, most likely they would become very inflamed by the opinion of the other and most likely walk out. This chapter is probably not for you if you are from one of those groups, unless you are willing to listen to differing viewpoints. This chapter is for the people who find themselves unsure about the subject because they recognize there is an element of truth in just about everything.

I almost hesitate to talk about these subjects because I don't want to tell people what to think, but I have been communicating with the Ascended Masters and asking questions my entire life and I believe there may be some people who could use a little basic, non-inflammatory thoughts about these things. I personally have always felt as though I had an intimate relationship with Christ Jesus. I further believe that I may be speaking for the silent majority, whereas the folks who are very polarized on these subjects could be considered the vocal minority. I noticed that when one person speaks, it primes the pump for others who may have been hesitant to speak up.

Very often, members of the soul family, Archangel Michael are likely to have an instinctual knowledge of Christ Jesus. This is because we share a communal history.

The Holy Bible has some good things in it that resonate with other esoteric teachings, but it is not perfect because it has been written by humans and translated and manipulated throughout time.

Church can be a good place to start for some people, but the real altar of truth lies in a purified heart and healed instinctive center. We are fallible beings and although we should not make excuses, we were forgiven before we came here. Discernment is our individual responsibility – this is not something another is can do for us.

If you would like to expand your understanding of the man, Jesus, I suggest you do some reading and see if you find resonance in other material. The Book of Urantia and The Book of Mormon are good resources. A Course in Miracles is another book to check out if you want to get an expanded view of Jesus. The information in these books represent a much broader view of the man than is alluded to in most organized religion. You may also ask Christ Jesus to help you understand him.

Christ Jesus was one fragment of a soul group of 144,000, and others are destined to follow in his footsteps and achieve Christ Consciousness also. This is the primary reason I am writing this book – to wake up other Christed beings. The 144K have to align in order to create enough of an energetic pull that everything else ascends. We are destined to do this and so we must. This is the order of the karmic business because we are the oldest souls.

Christ Consciousness is Love, not a moral judgment.

It should be obvious that Jesus and the others in his soul group taught Love. I believe that is the main message in the Holy Bible as well. I believe anything other than that is a misinterpretation of the message. Very often people use the name of Jesus to judge others. This is not a correct interpretation of his teachings. 1 John 4:16 states "God is Love and he who abides in Love abides in God and God abides in him." It could not be simpler than this. Notice that it does not say that Jesus is Lord or that God is a man.

Some espouse the exact interpretation of all of the messages contained in the Bible. I suggest we first acknowledge that language has evolved as human civilization has evolved. All one needs to do is look at books or documents from 100 or 200 years ago and it is obvious that language was used differently only centuries earlier. We add words to our dictionary on a yearly basis. We group words differently as we evolve. We have developed a variety of shades of most of our words. Common sense tells me that the Bible is not a reliable, word for word, literal handbook for seekers of the truth, while it does have valid points. Most documents have both inaccurate and accurate elements.

Regarding Jesus as Lord and savior, if Jesus did tell people that he was God or Lord and that they should call on him and only on him as the singular way to God, then he was saying it because he knew that his omnipresent existence would direct their consciousness thusly, and steer them away from beings or idols that were not benevolent beings. We know from archeological and other sources that the people of the era of Jesus Christ were grappling with the subject of idols and Gods. It has been suggested that there were off-planetary beings messing with humanity and enamoring them with false powers. He was simply trying to direct them to spirituality 101. Focusing on Christ is only the beginning. Once we integrate our own connection to Christ Consciousness, we no longer need a crutch. The journey from there is infinite. It does not stop at Christ Jesus and the Holy Bible.

The spiritual new age is big on individual empowerment. Christ Jesus also told people that they had the power within and this can be found in numerous places in the Bible. One of my favorite pieces from the Bible is Psalm 40:8. I desire to do your will my lord. Your desire is in my heart. (NIV Bible) or I delight to do thy will, O my God: yea, thy law is within my heart. (KJV) It clearly states that an individual carries the instructions of the creative force within them. It does not direct people to an outside source for their answers and that includes your Bible!

The Holy Bible substantiates some of the most significant premises of the spiritual new age.

Throughout the Bible, writers also discussed the gifts of prophecy, etc. One of the parts of us that has been driven underground is our intuitive abilities. Without this we are not complete humans or extensions of creation. There is not one singular viewpoint on this subject in the text. For one to draw a conclusion based on one perspective offered therein is an attempt to use the authority of the Bible to bolster narrow-minded, ill-advised viewpoints.

In the end, my suggestion is that you should look for things that are repeated often, fit together with other things and resonate in your soul if you want to discern what to keep and what to throw away. I would like to see the day when people are so clearly connected to Source that they don't have to argue about the accuracy and reliability of external sources.

Once you understand how consciousness works, you can see why Christ Jesus told people to call on him for a connection to the real God, but you must understand that it is not the only way to connect with Source or God. Once you have established this level of consciousness within by becoming the embodiment of Love or by striving to become Love, it is not necessary.

However, if you want to use Jesus Christ as a focal point, I believe it is a valid and useful tool. So, don't turn away from Christ just because you don't believe he is Lord and

Savior and died for your sins. At the same time, I don't think it is wise to believe that all the answers are in the Bible or that the teachings in the Bible are the only ones God gave us.

It is understandable that people feel the need for a concrete, infallible source for answers. This place exists only in our pure connection to our soul. We've all walked away from spirit and now we are walking back. We are developing the tools to do this now. This is the primary reason we need to be passionate and forgiving.

Remember always, needing a focal point is spirituality 101. Your inner knowing is the Holy Grail.

Recommended Reading:

The Urantia Book (with an open and discerning mindset)

Spiritually Correct: Doing Away With One-Size-Fits-All Spirituality

Humans have searched since the dawn of time to find a Golden outline or nomenclature for spiritual practices. The integration of the spiritual into a world of form requires a level of mastership and we are working on some of the finishing touches – at the brink of a breakthrough – ready to experience a new era of harmony on Earth. When we read about spirituality, the concepts appear to be obvious and easy, yet it can be a daunting task to integrate spiritual practices into every day life here. The ultimate goal is to have one foot in the spiritual and one foot in the physical, allowing the spiritual to guide the physical. This requires knowledge of how the spiritual realms work and how they work through us.

We wish connecting to spirit would be as easy as knowing what food to eat and what kind of music to listen to, but it isn't. It takes trial and error to learn how it feels to be harmonized and in resonance with creation. This is the only human endeavor that can create peace within and without. All other goals keep us on an never ending treadmill.

I believe we have done a great job of understanding how the spiritual realms operate and what the intended outcome is, but we haven't necessarily done so well in putting all of this into practice because we continue to want to assign lifestyle habits and personality traits to spirituality.

There is more flexibility in practices in the physical realm than there is in the spiritual. I think we have been focusing too much on the physical and attempting to validate our spirituality by applying physical attributes to attainment. The focusing and refinement is being misapplied because there is a level of compromise on the physical level, whereas there is not compromise on the spiritual level because we did not create that level. Our limiting human perspectives cause us to create strong judgments around success, health, and beauty because we seem to have a strong need to label things.

The ascension spiral is a very individual climb and it isn't always pretty. What happens when we attempt to get a picture of what spiritually correct is, we create another set of egotistical goals and judgments, further keeping our hearts and spirits in lock down. *A Course in Miracles* urges us to let go of judgment – not labeling things as good or bad. Good and bad are ego judgments. Sometimes doors close so that we can be led to a better place and sometimes really "bad" things happen to bring us to our eternal perspective. It is best to let spirit guide us and inform us each singular step along the way. One of the first things that newbie spiritual seekers adopt is to trust in the process or the flow.

Throughout time, the ego has used God and spirituality to justify its own means. Many an organized group or religion has claimed to be the saved ones. Groups have harbored spiritual secrets and powers, created symbols and codes, etc. Many people have broken away from regimented religion and as such now call themselves spiritual. However, spirituality has not escaped ego based mental traps.

The general outline of a spiritualist these days has come to be one who believes in the legalization of marijuana, the existence of ET's, channeling, psychic phenomenon, Reiki, being vegan/vegetarian, expecting the government to take care of the populous and making sure the wealthy pay their share and so on. We have once again designated a set of behavioral traits as a Golden outline for access to spirit – merely changing the disguise. Real spirituality lies in the heart and what is actualized and integrated in that space. Without Love or higher consciousness, nothing is of lasting value no matter what.

Unfortunately, many of these behaviors do not accomplish the goal of strengthening our connection to spirit and therefore cannot be guideposts on the road to spirituality. Although we often come up with behaviors that do in fact hold an element of spiritual truth, most of what people have come up with during this spiritual revolution amount to, as Marianne Williamson would frame it, "...rearranging deck chairs on the Titanic."

We connect most accurately with our spirit by becoming the embodiment of Love, living in the moment and taking inspired action

To be spiritual, one must be of spirit and follow their spirit. Let your spirit choose for you; not your ego – sounds simple, but it requires practice. This is very personal and it involves a great deal of trial and error, so it is natural that we will be tripped up as we learn a new way of living and interacting with the world and others.

Outside of this golden outline, that which we enjoy for entertainment, the foods we eat, and activities we partake in, the challenges we are willing to face, our blueprint, our path, our destiny, our sexuality, and much of the rest is our own damn business. Naturally, it is extremely beneficial to be vigilant of our addictive tendencies. I only mention this to caution against creating another bucket list of things to be judgmental about. If we get back to the metaphysical basics of spiritual connection – centered, grounded, in the moment, coming from Love – and be patient enough to allow our soul to show us the rest, we will correct our paths as well as our thinking. It can be challenging to understand the difference between a spiritual discipline and a ritual or behavior. A spiritual discipline is an actual practice that will eventually lead us to our spirit – such as stilling the mind. It has been scientifically demonstrated that stilling the mind allows one to access intuition and creativity, which are of the spirit. Mediums and professional intuitives know that they have to still their mind in order to connect.

Rituals are generally human made activities that may or may not lead us to our spirit. Many earlier spiritual practices and many practices from organized religion would be considered rituals. They are benign – neither here nor there. You may take them or leave them or make up your own. Many things are multi-faceted and most times evade one size fits all answers.

One subject that sheds a great deal of light on this subject is veganism/vegetarianism. There are those who embrace veganism/vegetarianism because they feel lighter, healthier and morally justified, yet studies of individual physical and blood types demonstrate that some bodies require meat in order to survive. Those who resonate with the vegetarian diet have difficulty understanding that others have encountered serious health issues when they went on such a diet. There are people in my social circles who have died or became very ill as a result of vegan or raw diets because their genetic make up did not support it. In other words, it is best to see diet as a scientific thing rather than a spiritual thing.

The interesting thing about the subject of vegetarian vs carnivore is there are some things with regard to spiritual truth that do come into play here – but it is not what you may think it is. I have discovered that historically, we adopted belief systems because they did in fact bring us in line with critical scientific or spiritual laws – although we may not have known why at the time.

For instance, we do not believe in incest and although we have come to believe this is a moral directive, it is actually a scientific directive because of the natural law - survival of the fittest. In order for this law to operate, gene pools must continually merge with other gene pools to insure the evolution of an ever-stronger version of any designated species. This applies to animals as well as humans.

To assure this happens, we all have signature pheromone scents that are subtly infused with a smell designed by our specific genes. Pheromones contain quantum level magnetic factors, which should repel or attract others whose gene pools would mesh well with our own. We are programmed to reject pheromones from our own gene pool and therefore should not be sexually attracted to our close relatives. Animals perpetuate their species similarly. Homosexual people are predisposed to reject the pheromones of the opposite sex and desire the pheromones of the same sex.

Many of the behaviors that we deem spiritual or moral are actually scientifically based or may be examined from a scientifc perspective for greater clarity.

In the same way, it may not be a matter of whether one eats meat or not; it appears to be a matter of which animals were predestined by grand design for our consumption and which ones were not. The reason that some animals are destined to be consumed by humans and others are not is that some have come here to evolve just as we do, and some have come here to be part of the food chain. There are some passages in the

Bible, Kosher guidelines and teachings of the Tao ti ching that substantiate this thinking. As I mentioned earlier, we often don't know exactly why we have adopted certain habits or why. The reasons for the choices in this instance appear to be both spiritual and scientific.

The teachings of the Tao ti ching state that animals with a cloven hoof are those with cluster souls and are meant for human consumption because they incarnated here for the purpose of feeding us. When you eat a chicken or a cow, you are consuming an animal that has a cluster soul. Plucking one cow or chicken from the field is like picking a piece of fruit from a tree. You do not kill the tree by taking a piece of fruit because you are not consuming or killing the vessel. Cluster animals are the same in that there is one soul expressed through many animals.

The teachings of the Tao ti ching say that we are not to consume animals with non-cloven hooves such as horses. These animals have individual souls with an evolutionary spiral of their own. Animals with paws are also included in the types of animals that have an individual soul and should be respected as such. This of course includes rabbits, cats, dogs, etc.

The Tao ti ching coincides with the teachings that Christ Jesus taught as stated in the Bible. He also stated that we could only consume animals with a cloven hoof and were not to eat those with a paw. He did not say why, but the Tao ti ching explains this well. These are different facets of the same human issue. Do you see the value of introspection and being open minded enough to peer into many religions? I also believe these to be solid derivations because in my heart, I feel a strong resonance. I have never felt that I wanted to eat a rabbit or a dog – as most do not. As always, I suggest you do your own research and meditation on this.

To get an idea of where humans were at when some of the earlier spiritual disciplines were established, it is important to remember that earlier humans were very barbaric as a result of the need to put survival above all else. Once we were able to become more adept at survival, we needed to begin to shed our animal instincts and become more conscious of a few things until we arrived at the next level of spiritual development. What was necessary at one point in our evolution, no longer serves us once we have risen to a higher level. Furthermore, a deeper spiritual truth can be accessed through a disciplined practice, but the practice is temporary at best and should be held onto loosely to allow for even more spiritual growth.

Now that we have gotten better at survival, we evolve to embrace a higher level of trust in spirit & living with a high level of authenticity, joy and freedom.

So, evolving is not a matter of changing our behavior; it is a matter of going deeper into our hearts to find the authentic self. Then, all of our personal choices and priorities will come from this place and should be trusted. We need to stop being so confused if we are to live a more joyful life. If we accept that a spiritual path leads to bliss, then the question remains, what is in the way of our bliss? This is where it gets tricky. We all have a cosmic disposition, unique soul history and goals, and earthly personality and recent history. When it comes to repairing the connection and cleaning up the debris, there is no one size fits all approach. One cannot simply talk the talk, listen to a certain kind of music and use a certain type of soap and become healed. So, what do we do?

Each individual harbors different challenges and it has come to a point where so many people's systems are so jammed up, they are most likely going to need help from others to get back into integrity. It is going to take the work of thousands of energy workers and intuitives in order to guide individuals to locate and heal poor programming or blockages. I believe that is why many intuitives and other energy workers have surfaced at this time and are offering their help to others. It is a time to be advocating for the licensing and legitimization of energy workers.

In the absence of a professional or voluntary intuitive, we all have etheric help available and we all may find our way back to our instinctive center – it is our birthright. The energy loves to transmute and heal things. All energy is programmed to ascend, just as our bodies are designed to seek homeostasis. We need to get out of the way and release our attachment to dense and discordant energies and allow Source energy to put us back together.

This essentially is what is meant by surrender. Surrender is the loosening of the confines of the dense physical aspects of our identity/struggles and the infusion of the lighter spiritual energies of our etheric body. We make the choices to let go and nobody can do this for us. We can't do it for anybody else either.

During these turbulent times we may feel that we are on the brink of something, yet we teeter between two worlds. It is hard to leave behind what was familiar and move into something entirely new. Many of the big dreams and ideas we have when we are feeling lighter and connected to spirit are things that, if we believed in them and accepted them, would come to fruition. The Universe will jump in and help us with if we allow our lives to be used to manifest the heretofore unmanifested. This is the creative potential we must release into the earth realm.

*The spiritual path may seem too easy
or too good to be true*

until we realize this is the new normal.

One of things we often do when we feel helpless and confused is that we reach out to our family or friends. Unfortunately, many of them are dealing with their own stuff and often seeing through muddied lenses. Most often, people will see something from their own past experiences, which has nothing to do with another person's journey. Please don't despair when this occurs. I am not trying to put a wedge in friendships and relationships; I am supplying you with tools that will help you in the darkest of moments, when you feel utterly alone and lost. The reality is, we all have moments when we only have our intuition and angelic help to guide us. I believe that suicidal thoughts come up most for people when they feel cornered with no place to turn. It is at times like these that we must learn to go within. Please understand that there is ALWAYS an answer. These dark nights of the soul are chrysalis moments. Feeling hopeless simply means we have relinquished all previous solutions and it is time to find the Golden answers.

The ascent or return to full spiritual actualization begins with intent and then the energy works with the individual to reveal the unique blueprint

The ascent or return to full spiritual actualization begins with intent. The intent may be conscious or subconscious. The intent to become aligned with our soul creates a higher vibrating burst of energy in our energy field. The color of this vibration will be at minimum a violet color. This is the minimum vibration required to begin the clearing of all misguided, mis-qualified, discordant energy in our energy field. Metaphysically, violet functions as cosmic Draino. It is the strongest energy and therefore it trumps other energies. It begins to push the discordant energy out. This is why some people believe that all you have to do is decide to live the life of your spirit in order to live a spiritually driven life. To a certain extent, this is true because of the transmutation qualities of higher energies. There is a big initial shift and then all the stuff begins to be purged. This is why some people flip the switch and have some epiphanies and then believe it is a done deal. It is kind of like giving birth to a baby. Once the hormones have shifted and the body begins the process of giving birth, it is almost certain that the baby will come out. However, in many circumstances, assistance is needed in order to complete the process.

There is such a significant change when we decide to live a spiritual life, but the initial impact and opening is only the beginning. It is easy to see why people get stuck. It is common to hang on to old ways without knowing it. There are conscious and subconscious reasons that people often say they are stuck or feel that they want more. We plateau on a regular basis. We need to become accustomed to constantly rising. It is good to recognize when we are stuck. Abraham speaking through Esther Hicks says, "You will never get it done and you can never get it wrong." Every little thing that we do to experience joy and every little thing we do to raise our vibration, feels so much better than the last moment, we should not want to stop. We are designed as ever expanding beings, just as the Universe also expands.

Karma From the Perspective of Akasha

I will be explaining how karma looks from a higher perspective and how the law of attraction works with regard to our creations in the realm of Akasha. Because I have had my ancient eyes open since I was a child, I have been able to observe the human predicament for a very long time. Because of my vibrational status, I am able to receive information about just about anything by accessing a band of consciousness known as the Akashic Records. Much of what we have been led to believe about karma is not completely accurate so I feel the need to clarify it during this karmic cleanup time.

Akasha is a band of consciousness that is part of the blend that we bring to the creative canvas and it functions on the Law of Attraction just like anything else. As it is a part of our energy cache, it will attract the karmic relationships we need to balance our karma. It can't be avoided, but it can be purified. Please allow it to show you your imbalances so you may fix them. Identify, analyze and purify the issue and got on with the good things. The types of relationships and the life you attract will change as a result.

Karma is not the simplistic method of payback that we have been led to believe in some cases. It is much more complicated than that. It has to do with quantum entanglement. Karma creates our experience and perception. For instance, if we are dishonest inside our self, we will not perceive honesty/dishonesty correctly on the outside.

Also, The spiritual new age is big on creating the life of our dreams; that is putting the cart before the horse. I don't believe enough is said in general about cleaning up karma. The "dream board" will change once we reach higher consciousness. We can create the life of our dreams when we clear up enough of our karma. Until then, our perception is too muddy to co-create our dream lives.

It is hard to know what it is exactly that we want and how to choose when we are carrying around data from our past and from others. Thoughts and feelings create just as planets do through the laws of attraction. Many of our thoughts and feelings come from our past and from others in our energetic space.

Akasha is an ever flowing and undulating river of consciousness that pervades everything just like the fields of the Archangels – it is omnipresent. Access to it has allowed me to see the basis of karmic struggles between people – a glimpse into things that are normally out of reach to us when we are in the midst of turmoil. It has shown me that everything here on Earth clusters in the same way that the planets did as they were forming.

We are simply living in a slowed down version of creation to allow for trial and error. It is all based on vibrations and the solidification of the highest energetic combinations that are eternally blown apart to provide for even higher vibrating clusters. This is how evolution occurs on all levels of creation.

Everything that is created, regardless of the vibration, is connected through quantum entanglement. There is never a moment when we are not creating, so it is easy to imagine the size of the debris field that has resulted from our mis-creations. Some people will have to walk through a void or a time period when not much is going on in their life until they transform everything in their fields and bodies into unconditional Love.

Karma is anything that is not in highest energetic integrity – which is Christ Consciousness.

The events of our lives are most often not what they seem to be. Perceiving and processing all of our experiences through the lens of unconditional Love – the viewpoint of our higher self – aligns us with our highest energetic integrity – allowing us to move through events with greater wisdom and clarity. Engaging the distorted view of the lower self creates karma.

In order to feel comfortable in the fifth dimension, we have to bring ourselves into at least a minimal level of vibrational integrity by healing our past. Making the choice to become authentic will often trigger the re-living of events from our past in order to re-process them with a higher goal in mind. Feeling at peace with self and all else is the goal. The reason things come back to visit us is that all of our creations are connected to us through quantum entanglement. They will keep coming back for purification.

In this chapter, I will be examining the many ways we

create and how karma shows up in our lives – and how to get past it and get on with co-creation.

We have self-karma, relationship karma and group karma. Our self-karma bleeds into our relationship karma and then our relationship karma bleeds into our group karma.

Self Karma

Self karma is all the inner self talk and subconscious processing that reflects the way in which our unique pre-disposition has caused us to internalize our experiences. Everybody experiences and perceives things differently, based on their unique inherent qualities and past karma. Too much of a pile up creates a jaded and heavy existence. We will never have inner peace and peaceful relationships until we face our ill-programming.

Relationship karma encompasses all of our interactions with others who join us on our journey. When we are incomplete, we attract others who will highlight that imbalance. Once our imbalances are healed, we may enjoy synergistic relationships. Synergy is the goal of creation.

It is very difficult to have a relationship with the world until we get through our karmic relationships of a smaller nature. Nonetheless, the way we view God and all of creation will be an out-picturing of our inner world. The clearer our inner vision is, the clearer the events of the world will be.

While it is true that we attract better relationships when we are more authentic, all relationships are used to help us hone our clarity so avoidance and blaming will block the process of self-realization. Spiritual seekers learn that people and things are attracted to our energy because there is a karmic match. What ever comes into our lives is there for us to handle, not avoid.

Once again, only mindful living, introspection, slowing down, taking quiet time, will provide the necessary insights into our daily relational experiences. The subject is so specific and individual it is impossible to use a broad stroke to explain how to rectify things. A high quality energy worker or intuitive should be able to see the unique facets of all situations.

Why does karma occur to begin with? It stems from our original descent into matter or disconnection from God. Why do we seem to be endlessly in search of something? Why do we become so easily addicted? We yearn for our connection, yet we look outward instead. The separation exists only in our minds.

Born into the once low vibrating world of form, we are trained by society to be outwardly focused instead of being tapped into the unmanifested or creative force within. This is the source that feeds us and sustains us and creates new pathways. We are here to create from this place and nobody told us that. We must return our consciousness to Source/God.

We have become so disconnected from Source that we feel incomplete and we attract relationships to give us that missing sense of completion. When those replacements for inner peace fail us – and they will, we believe that it is someone or something else that is causing us to feel like we have been short-changed or harmed. We lash out, bicker, complain, blame and take others down with us. When we are engaged in struggles, we are not effective vehicles of co-creation.

The entire world is a reflection of our individual and communal imbalances and dysfunctions. Essentially, we are all to blame for society's woes. So, when it comes to resurrecting the environment and the government, we begin by sweeping in front of our own door. The spiritually actualized person is able to get past all the drama and take a leadership role in society.

Relationship Karma:

The way the Law of Attraction works in karmic relationships is the imbalances in us create a magnetic draw to the imbalances in others because all matter is programmed to seek completion. In the same way that elements that form planets are destined and designed to attract into something greater than their separate parts, so too are humans designed to become whole. Modern day spirituality has effectively taken a detour from the real work we need to do by encouraging us to seek our perfect "soul mate." The truth is, we have many, many soul mates. We will attract the ones that will spur the growth we need at any given time.

You know that feeling when you meet someone and you sense that you know them on a deep level or from another lifetime? The fact of the matter is you probably do know them from past lives as well as on so many other levels. This does not mean that you have found the love of your life and have to remain tied to them forever. Most often, this feeling is the introduction of a karmic relationship. The stronger the attraction, the more karmic it is.

Yes, in most cases Love exists on some level in the relationship, but most imbalanced relationships in the old paradigm were actually Love/Hate relationships. The attractiveness of Love is usually the first thing that brings us together with cosmic soul mates and it is the strongest feature of the relationship, so it shows itself in the initial stages. This is commonly known as the honeymoon stage. However, the same energy that brings us together brings with it all the rest of the baggage.

As I am trying to demonstrate, the purpose of the karmic relationship is to highlight all the baggage and morph everything into unconditional Love. What happens very often is people start the power struggles and blaming and then the relationships goes on a serious downward spiral.

When we blame instead of highlighting and correcting, we polarize and the issues become much worse than they were at the beginning. Many times, one of the participants in a relationship makes a decision to climb, while the other does not. This is the juncture when the parties tend part ways. All too often, the one who makes the initial decision to leave gets blamed – but there should be no blame. Our relationships are there for our growth, so we should instead thank the soul mate that came into our lives to help us grow. This is the best way to heal and continue on our journey with unconditional Love.

I think the toughest part of doing intuitive readings for people is helping them to understand that the person they believe they are in Love with is not their life partner, but a soul mate that has come to help teach the lessons of Love. It is always best to find the lessons and work on those before we walk away. Law of attraction will cause the same dynamics to revisit us over and over until we resolve them.

Group Karma:

How did all this karma begin in the first place? Understanding this is the key to forgiveness in my estimation. Reality has changed throughout the existence of humanoid beings on Earth, for many different reasons. There have been ascended civilizations that were very advanced technologically and spiritually. Some of these advanced civilizations lived together in total and utter peace.

Human inhabitants have gone through change and metamorphosis throughout our existence and no group or being corners the market on anything. We have loved and hated, built and destroyed; we have been oppressed and we have been the oppressors; we have been slaves and we have enslaved others; we have been both the victim and the murderer. It has been one hell of a cycle, yet a very short one in relation to the length of time Earth has been under construction.

This juncture is monumental because we are rehashing and reliving our human drama once again as we clear it out of the Akashic records. There are no victims or perpetrators. We must forgive and stop making the same mistakes.

We are loaded up with karma and very confused because of our communal past. If we keep nit picking and drudging up dirt, we will be stuck in the old dimension forever. The only way we are going to get over this huge energetic hump we have facing us is to be completely compassionate and forgiving. When we get all worked up about our petty issues and differences in the present moment, we can lose sight of the big picture. We bounce off of each other hundreds of times a day and we are confused about our behavior and that of others.

When we lose our inner vision we cannot see others for who they really are. In all karmic relationships it takes a really big person to side step the drama and power struggles and call a truce. This takes place when one decides its just going to be about Love from now on. It is time for us to get reconnected to our Source energy so we can end the karmic cycle. I believe this is one reason we have shorter lives right now than we have had in earlier cycles. Karmic cycles cause us to have to do more work than play and we have to keep recycling our physical body in order to do the necessary work. Again, the necessary work comes from recognizing where we are personally lacking in wholeness.

Esther Hicks channeling Abraham would say that we should embrace our constant desires because that is how we are designed. Yes, we are designed to be creators of ever increasing juiciness, as Esther says. I am talking about the side of us that often presents as beings that are cranky, neurotic, fidgety, compulsive, insomniacs who can't focus on anything, let alone co-creation. There is a distinct difference between spiritual longing and egotistical insatiability. Spiritual desires create inner peace, while ego desires create addiction.

Karmic history hits the 144K harder than others. These people have soul recall from times when the earth was peaceful, yet they have accumulated mountains of karma in the recent cycles of evolution or de-evolution. They have been through the most incarnations and have the potential for great leadership once their vast karmic history is clear. Through quantum entanglement, this soul group can single handedly redirect the course of Earth.

This group needs to step up and move surely up the ascension ladder and then everybody else will follow. When this energy is stabilized on Earth once again, it will be the dominant energy and will serve to transmute and cause everything else to rise. Herein lies the paradigm shift in the minds of humans. When a certain number of people reach a high enough level, all inhabitants will rise.

We are the ones we have been waiting for.

Unconditional Love begins with our own being. Then that transfers to our relationships. Once we accept and align with our authentic self, unconditional Love for others is automatic. It cannot occur the other way around. The process of resolving karma and becoming our authentic spiritual self is the evolutionary mandate we are participating in now and it is the priority. The third dimension is closed for business and you if feel stuck, it is time to rise.

The coming generations will experience longer, healthier, more joyous lives if we lay the necessary pathways.

We may not live to see all of the wonderful changes that are coming, but in our hearts we know what to do to bring the planet back into integrity. That's our purpose.

I recommend Jose Stevens books to get ideas about soul groups and soul mate relationships. I have never come across anything better than his work. Second to his books, I recommend Carolyn Myss and Mona Lisa Schulz if you are looking for insights into karmic relationship resolution.

Act Your Soul Age: Energy Integrity for the Old Soul

All humans are bombarded with energies of various types on a daily basis. This poses a particularly challenging problem for older souls and healers because they are inherently more sensitive. Lately, you may have heard the terms empaths and sensitives used more frequently because this group of humans are having the most difficulty staying balanced as the energies become more chaotic.

We old souls have learned from our large number of incarnations that we are at our core, one being, and that we are all in this together. Many including myself have a belief that we can only be happy when others are happy. While these compassionate attributes make for very good caregivers, we may be absolutely horrible at taking care of ourselves. Consequently, it may become very difficult to carry out our life plan. In my later years, I began to suffer health problems that have the signature injuries indicative of spending all of my energy for the benefit of others.

Many loving, caring, giving people will suffer the illnesses and energy imbalances that are part of the territory, but tools can be learned to keep these issues at bay or even reverse them.

In the same way that we are more sensitive spiritually, we are also more sensitive physically. Our nervous systems were created to be more sensitive intentionally. For instance, when I do readings for people, I listen to their voice. A less sensitive person would hear pretty much one sound coming out of the individual, but I hear an orchestra of sounds – each one carrying with it a vibrational quality that tells me much about that person – from their soul history to their current life imprinting. Because it is part of my life purpose to be a clairaudient being, I came in with highly sensitive tuning.

I also use this sensitivity to discern musical sounds. While less sensitive person would be duly influenced by the voice of another, they would not be in the position of discernment and therefore subject to misinterpretation of what they are receiving. Everything in our repertoire has its advantages and disadvantages. Physical sensitivities will also make us more easily ruffled and edgy than the common person. This is all the more reason to prioritize self-care and quiet time.

When a sensitive person engages with another, they join with their energy, even if it is just briefly. This merging allows for deeper understanding that goes beyond simple words. On the flipside, lack of communication comes from being too distanced and over-agendized. As a empaths and intuitives, we are fine tuned to many more things than the average person, with the downside being that we tend to take on outside energies more than others. The antidote is to learn how to move back into our individual alignment after we merge with another.

In order to do the things that we are programmed to

do in order to help raise the vibration of the planet, we sometimes step down our frequency, share our energy, flash or merge with the energy of others and even transmute the energies around us. It is ok that we do these things, but we must always make sure we fill ourselves up before we begin our day, limit the amount of time we spend taking on other energies and always make sure we take restorative breaks. We must never allow ourselves to become so submerged in earth energies that they begin to break us down and cause us to develop illnesses.

Because we are organic beings whose cells are designed to seek homeostasis, we can experience a certain level of abuse and neglect because our bodies will self-correct. This may cause us to take our health for granted for a period of time. However, as time goes on, our bodies lose the ability to bounce back quickly as many of us have experienced with each decade we advance in age. While we are blessed with these features that make us more able to help and work with others, we need to learn how to take care of these very delicate and tricky to balance instruments.

A clear and integral energy alignment requires that our mental, physical, emotional and spiritual bodies are working together in harmony. Each body has its own care prescriptions, which I will go into shortly. The mind should be clear and light, the physical body should feel balanced and comfortable, the emotional body should be brilliant and warm and the spiritual body should be radiating through all the other systems. This might seem kind of fussy, but the stronger we are in this regard, the better we are able to handle our life purpose and the increasingly difficult energies of the planet.

The best place to begin is to have a day or two, or perhaps a vacation away from all the stresses of life. It is important to establish an energy integrity baseline. What I mean by this is that we need to have a high vibrating energetic alignment that we can imprint as our reference point in order to know when we are off balance and also to help us know how off balance we are or how aligned we are. I realize that some people may not even know what it feels like to be in a very good and pure energetic space. Some other people may have many experiences of being in a very clear energetic space, yet they find themselves off balance at intervals. The important thing is to know how it feels to be aligned, how we get knocked off balance and what it takes to get back into alignment.

It will be difficult to come into alignment or even become aware of the alignment of the subtle bodies if the physical body is not healthy. I suggest that each person assess their imbalances by slowing down and listening to their mind, body and spirit. If the spirit is calling and we are not listening, there will be a constant nagging feeling. If the body is asking for help, it will feel ill or heavy or painful in given areas. It is advisable to take some quiet time and make an assessment. Write things down if that helps. Either way, understand that the physical body is the place where all other things become manifest, so it must be taken care of.

Everybody has a different ability to clear and get into his or her own personal, clear space. After much practice, I have gotten very adept at moving quickly into the restoration mode and getting back into alignment. It took dogged determination, education and practice to do so.

For some, it is a matter of moving away from stress and stressful situations and people and for others it can take more work. Nature has a tremendous ability to restore our mind and spirit. Unfortunately, when people use alcohol and drugs to deal with stress, they not only damage their physical body, but they open up their energy to an onslaught while they are taking a momentary break from the physical impacts of the stress in life.

I believe everybody should know what it is that works best to bring them back into the fold. Some may use peaceful music or breath work. Some may go to an energy practitioner. Exercise is great for reducing stress and re-centering. Self-talk and neurolinguistic programing are very useful in creating a more positive perspective. In order to shake stressful or discordant energies, breathing is an absolute necessity while all other modalities are of individual preference. Regardless of the methodology, we must make clearing and centering a priority.

Clear Mental Body

In order for our brain to receive signals from our instinctive center, it needs to be healthy. Brain health requires proper nutrition, rest and exercise. A key nutritional source for proper brain health and function is essential fatty acids. We are just beginning to understand the importance and role of fat in our diets. For decades, fat has been misunderstood. Please consult your physician before making any significant dietary changes. Also, our brain, or any parts of our body for that matter require sufficient hydration, which provides the vehicle necessary for electrical and nerve transmission capabilities.

Our brain functions in varying states. We have beta, alpha, theta, delta and gamma. Beta is the typical high speed that most people run on. Alpha is relaxed alert awareness. Theta is a state of deep relaxation or light sleep. Delta is a state of deep sleep, but is also available to those who are adept at reaching this state and being awake at the same time. Gamma is a state of very high awareness and rapid movement, most likely used for video gaming and possibly sports. In the higher brain wave states, one is entirely focused outward.

Because our brains process and store massive amounts of information, we need to give them adequate time to rest. During active times, it is best to keep our brains operating at lower oscillations to prevent overload. We need to learn how to run them slower and we also should avoid multitasking as much as possible. This is however, a learned ability. Using alcohol or drugs to slow down the brain is not advisable, because of the eventual damage that is done by overuse of substances that our body is not designed to process naturally. The same highs can be reached without side effects if one learns how to stay in an alpha/theta brainwave state. The body becomes relaxed and the warmth of the spirit is enjoyed by all of the senses when the brain is not cranking and doing over time. There are no side effects involved in becoming centered – only benefits.

We cannot respond to our instinctive center when our brain is in beta. We do not have intuition of any kind when we are in this state. We are in the state of responding to outside stimuli and this has become the accepted norm. From a spiritualist viewpoint, this state is referred to as "being in your head." It is what causes headaches, frustration, anger and human separation and conflict.

Normally, we are in alpha/theta upon waking. The ideal state is to be in alpha/theta with consciousness centered in the feeling center or heart.

A good spiritual practice should help to remove old, worn out and negative programming from the brain. If the past was loaded with negativity and it is still being carried around and accessed on a daily basis, all the good stuff will not be able to come forth, nor will it even be recognized as such. There are plenty of spiritual books on the market to help you with this type of clearing. I like to use talk therapy for this myself.

Clear Emotional Body

The emotional body is of utmost importance in the overall physical and spiritual health of the individual. This is the place where the spirit flows into the body and it is the part of us that senses the initial impulses of our soul. If we were to have complete energetic autonomy and not be a slave to society or the system, we would have to have a clear instinctive center. Our soul knows exactly what to do, what to know and how to carry it out its desires, but most of us have blocked communication as the result of lifetimes of stuffing and ignoring the promptings we have received.

Life has been difficult if not harsh for many. Most of us have not been able to express ourselves or live with the joy that we are meant to live with. The pain that we have experienced can be stored in our heart centers, causing us to be jaded and shut down emotionally. If we go through the process of forgiving our self and others for the pain we are carrying around, we can experience the joy of life once again. The joy is always there and it awaits our return if we are willing to let go of the past. There is almost no one on this earth who has not been hurt or stifled.

A large part of the spiritual movement has been focused on healing the heart and learning to love. The ability to be in touch with the soul is the reason for it. Without the healing of the heart, the spirit cannot guide us and fill us up.

Being Grounded

Grounding is a confusing term and it can come across as not too much fun either. Actually, having the bodies working together is part of grounding. When the physical, mental and emotional bodies are healthy, clear and working in harmony together, the spirit can work through them to carry out our life purpose and provide for a joyful, blissful experience.

The next part of grounding is being here and fully aware and in the moment. Whenever we think about the future, the past or some other place or person, we are not completely in our bodies. While we may be very well attached to our heart centers, we may be transporting our self consciously somewhere else. This is not figurative. We literally exist where we place our consciousness.

Being in the moment has significant energetic benefits. Everything in creation is eternally expanding and rising. Therefore, any missteps others as well as our selves have made, when held onto, hold us back. As soon as we let go of the past and get in the moment, all of the good things we missed will find us once again.

We should always be giving and receiving in equal measure, which is tricky. Theoretically or metaphysically speaking, everything on our path should be taken care and move along smoothly of if we stay grounded and centered and in the moment.

As spiritual elders, we must cultivate and practice impeccable self-care practices. Not only is it suggested, it is necessary because we suffer more readily than others when we don't stay aligned due to our high level of sensitivity. Above all else, never forget that Love is your strength, guidance and protection. It should be your go-to place.

Earth is designed to be an Angel's paradise. It is a place where Angels come to play and interact with others in harmony.

Always remember, laughter is the highest vibration. Have fun.

Crystal Clear: Energetic Freedom

It is your God given right and choice to have energetic independence and to keep your aura clear and healthy at all times. There is no obligation as a light bringer to take on or transmute discordant energy. When you achieve energetic independence, you are energetically free from menacing karmic cords and life draining energy connections. As an energetically independent individual, you are free to flow with your spirit as it is guided by divine will and grand design. Spirit will then direct you to those things where your energy and unique gifts will be most effective.

Higher Consciousness/Christ Consciousness/Love is your resting place no matter what the circumstances.

As an instrument of Heaven, our priority must be to align with higher consciousness/Love and to be as clear and unfettered as possible. We must take good energetic, physical, emotional and mental care of our selves no matter what and be sure not to get caught up in the turmoil of society. We should be able to look at everything that is going on in the world and keep a cool head about it and never forget the spiritual truth about things.

This is not to say that we are not supposed to help others. When we release the karmic ties, we are then led to serve in the best way possible for others as well as our self. In most cases, our role in helping others is to be as loving, authoritative and to the point as we can be. We are not supposed to hang around and become a crutch.

For most of us, our purpose is much bigger than we believe it to be and playing small and getting hooked into small human drama schemes is not wise. Furthermore, getting caught up by the small stuff can cause life threatening illnesses due to our highly sensitive nature; a critical thing to keep in mind.

We have often made contracts and agreements with other souls in between lives that are not serving us or anyone else for that matter. There are roles we play in our family groups. We are often afraid to hurt others and want to save people from themselves, but we must keep in mind, what is good for one is good for all. Although it may feel like we are obligated, we are not required to allow anyone to attach to our energy and use us as an anchor or be used as a scapegoat. The guilt we hold in our subconscious (borne of group karma) makes us believe this is so. We are not security blankets nor are we responsible for anybody's growth or guidance, unless we are responsible for small children.

Guilt and other karmic agendas make us feel on the deeper levels that we must hold others up. We begin to heal by becoming aware that we are doing this. Then we need to search for the hidden or obvious reasons why we are allowing others to use our energy and then we need to do the necessary healing or clearing. We have self-karma, relationship karma and group karma that keeps us trapped in this holding pattern. We are intended to experience joy while uplifting the energy on the planet with our joyful service. If we are tired and drained, we are rendered useless to our self or anyone else. We are not intended to be martyrs.

Although our purpose is large, we always have to be mindful that we don't interpret things through the ego. In *The Book of Urantia* there is a suggestion that the Violet race bred with the lower functioning beings on the planet in order to accelerate the advancement of the same. I think this is interesting because it sounds like something we would do out of spiritual ego – overreaching our abilities and purpose – with a destructive result.

This summation is also in synch with other stories about the evolution of human like species on Earth. If you do your research, there are many postulations about our evolutionary history. As always, I suggest one study these historical accounts with an open mind and a great dose of discernment. Look for the commonalities. Take what you will and store the rest for later. I especially like to see the commonalities that arise when scientific studies match spiritual memories and documents.

You may have had dreams that reveal the history of this soul family.

We also have karmic guilt from the times when we were feared for our spiritual power and knowledge in part because we handled ourselves in a misguided fashion. During the gothic period and the times of the crusades and the significant activity of the Knights Templar (1000 AD to 1600 AD), the struggle to keep Christianity alive through the over zealous use of force appears to have been self-defeating.

The true redemptive powers of Christian spiritual laws were driven underground in order to protect Christianity's interests. As a result, centuries of secrecy have damaged and distorted image of Christianity and everything that it stands for. The value and meaning of Christ is all but completely destroyed. All of these distortions are the result of a left-brain, male dominated interpretation of spiritual power.

We may forgive ourselves now for the history of these early Christians, and we do not need to continue to carry the shame and hide our lights anymore. We don't need to defend it anymore either. It is time to shine our lights and use Christ Consciousness in conjunction with the highest level of understanding and humility. We will use our lives this time around to correct the past by behaving differently, not carrying around karma.

Once we realign with our spiritual presence, we need to be patient as our true path and purpose unfolds. Notice too, that patience is a facet of Love. Above all else, our purpose is to function with energetic integrity in all that we do.

Love has a high enough vibration to transmute just about anything. The following chapter goes into the twelve aspects of divine Love. If all else fails, reboot by re-aligning with Love. Becoming aware of the aspects or facets will allow you to diagnose where you may be misaligned.

As we go through our day, we pick up energies and we make judgments that throw off our alignment and connection to spirit. Simply because we were in perfect alignment one day, it does not follow that we always are. Alignment feels light and joyful as though the wind is blowing through you, the mind is clear and open, energy is moving smoothly, positivity and creativity abound, and Love is within and without. Once you understand how to be in a high vibration, it is wise to begin and end each day being clear and centered rather than let discordant energy hang around for days, months or years. Because we are so sensitive, long periods of time being off balance may result in illness.

When our life force energy begins to slow down, our body begins to demise. It is never too late to begin to work on balancing and healing. When we begin to feel younger and more enthusiastic about life again, we know we have restored our youthful spirit.

We have our own residual past to clear out and we encounter the pain residual in others as we go about our business. How often have you had one glorious day or felt amazing when you woke up and by the end of the day, you were ready to crawl under a rock? Navigating in this chaotic world is still pretty tricky even though there is an awakening going on. The same awakening that will save us is forcing yucky stuff to come up over and over until we all become light once again. Be vigilant.

When we open ourselves up to larger energy systems (the public for instance) we feel all of that energy. Each advancement we make requires that we recalibrate and develop new filters. Filters are energetic adjustments that allow us to be free of interfering energies.

Even Wayne Dyer had trouble with the energies. He told me so. Be vigilant of agendas you may be carrying because they bump up against the agendas of others. God's will be done is win/win – no agenda.

The Love in our hearts and minds needs to be our go-to place when all else fails. Above all else, nurture and develop this energy so that you may use it for your anchor. Let this place feed you and sustain you. You are going to need it.

I recommend the book, *The Sovereign Soul: A Spiritual But Not Religious Woman's Guide to Living a Soul Centered Life* by Kaite McGrew.

Christ Consciousness Through the 12 Aspects of Spiritual Love

All quotes from *A Course in Miracles* are from the Second Edition, 1996, ©Foundation for Inner Peace, P.O. Box 598, Mill Valley, 94942-0598, www.acim.org and info@acim.org

Christ Consciousness and Ascension have been shrouded in an aura of mystery throughout the millennia. Simply stated, Christ Consciousness is unconditional Love the way that God intended it to be. Particularly in recent centuries, when spirituality was driven underground, this subject would have been considered taboo. Now experiencing a return to the forefront, the term strikes a nerve for the souls whose destination it was to start grasping the concept in this lifetime. There have been civilizations throughout the history of our planet that vibrated much higher than we do now. During those times of higher vibrations, beings on Earth lived in peace and harmony. We are about to become like that once more.

Ascension is a state of complete integration of Christ Consciousness.

The secrecy during the dark ages and human prejudices have played roles in the complication of this concept. To further complicate things, if you surf the web and check out YouTube videos, you will find thoausands of thoughts about Ascension and Christ Consciousness, many of which are distorted. All of this can be misleading and confusing, causing the subject to appear daunting or scary, when in fact it is life giving and beautiful.

Ascension is a high vibratory state where one is connected to the unified field, creative field, God or Source, providing a constant flow of life giving energy. It is a state of being connected to the soul – the authentic self. In this energy, we are guided, connected to eternal life, co-creators, accessing creative intelligence and in a state of peace and sometimes bliss. If accomplished communally, this would translate into a society that is harmonized and at peace.

The concepts of Ascension and Christ Consciousness actually have no basis in religious dogma as such. When we study the aspects of Love or the keys to Ascension, we are delving into the realm of unconditional Love, which is omnipresent and universal because it is the intelligence or creative force that created all that is. If all you do today is accept the fact that Love is the creative force and the only real power and make that your priority, you could throw this book away and be better off than most.

However, if you want to be really strong and live in the state of Heaven on Earth every day of your life, you will need to go deeper into this subject and really atone and refresh every aspect of your being. From there, creation will show itself to you more every day, so prepare to be amazed and enamored once again with life. Ascension is a process of spiritual rewind – the removal of all pre-dispositions created by the ego or the lower self. The ego is false identity and false personality based on the accumulation of imprinting from current and past lives. Ego creates a false perception of God's reality and blinds us to the magnanimous spiritual truth that belies all things.

In the most recent millennia, if one achieved a high vibration, they would become invisible to those in the lower planes. This does not need to happen any more because our planet is vibrating high enough to host Ascended beings once again. One may be Ascended and still be completely visible and functioning here on this beautiful planet. This is a great time to be alive. Beware however that the darkness would have you believe otherwise.

In this place of connection to our inner being, we are enamored with all aspects of life – from the seemingly insignificant to the challenging and the magnificent. When was the last time that you sat on the carpet and felt the texture of the fibers and let your body move as it may, with no rhyme or reason? Children do this. When was the last time you encountered a challenge and exclaimed, "I can do this?" When did you last jump in the car and drive off, not knowing where you were headed? Do you step outside and feel the grass under your feet and hear the birds singing in the trees, or are you so caught up in the list of things to do that you didn't even notice the bird's song? Our soul calls us but we do not listen.

Are you surprised to learn that all of this depth is a part of the Ascension process? Ascension is not the act of rising up and leaving the planet, it is the act of raising our vibrations to become more alive. When we look at the world, others and ourselves with an innocent perspective, we see the beauty – we see the miracle of creation. The issue prior to now is not only have we allowed our brains and minds to become programmed by the outdated, sluggish thinking of the masses, we are also carrying around discordant energy in our chakras from our ill-processed and internalized life experiences. We become reconnected with life only if we are willing to remove and heal the debris of our past programming. This process takes time and dedication. Just as we were trained away from our inner wisdom, we may train ourselves to return.

Our lives are meant to be a journey of discovery and ever deepening self awareness.

Unfortunately, from a very young age we are trained to focus outward. The act of focusing outward unplugs us from our soul and therefore disconnects us from God or Source. It causes us to become enamored with "false idols." When we are young and in school the authorities tell us to listen to them and pay attention to the blackboard or listen to their orders. This sets the stage for the first brainwashing we receive from society. When we get older, we watch the television, go to work and get lost on our electronic devices. Our list of things to do gets so enormous that we cannot sleep at night. We have trained ourselves to be a world of sleep deprived, walking zombies with no real direction. No wonder people are in need of so much comfort that they reach for drugs, alcohol, displaced anger, frustration and blame to try to ease the pain.

Who wrote the book of Love?

The force that created this Universe created the operating system and that operating system is Love. If I am to trust my inner guidance, the creative fabric of this Universe is Archangel Michael or Christ Michael. All of the Archangels and Christed beings are bands of consciousness and omnipresent. They are in essence, creative forces.

Christ Consciousness, Love and Ascension are words that are synonymous and inseparable. You may notice that I use the word God sparsely, because it is not a clearly defined term and has been distorted by people throughout time. It offends some people. The fact of the matter is God is Love and Love is God, but for most people this is not what God means, so I try to avoid it. Referring to creation as a metaphysical phenomenon rather than an animate object seems to be more acceptable and understandable to a larger group of people. At any rate, God is not a person, but a creative force – at least that is what I mean when I use the term.

Many souls, such as my self, have come to Earth from higher dimensions to be of assistance throughout time, but have lost their way and forgotten who they are. To a certain extent, most souls forget who they are when they get here because it is dense.

I went through a re-ascension process in the early 1990's, which I initiated by surrendering to God. With the help of *A Course in Miracles,* and countless hours of inner work – the proof was in the pudding. On my website, alanakay.com, there is an aura picture of myself that appears indigo and violet. The computer-generated description that accompanied this kirlian photograph described my energy as all ultra-violet, which is pure consciousness. My question with regard to making a choice from the numerous spiritual teachers out there, would be: Do you want to learn a subject from a person who has mastered a subject, or would you want to learn it from someone who is simply guessing or speculating about the subject? I am qualified by the Ascended Masters to teach Christ Consciousness because I have achieved the level of Christ Consciousness in this lifetime. This state is available to all souls and achievement is a process that begins with surrendering to your soul and accepting etheric help.

How the twelve aspects of Love came to me...

When I write, I am guided by my soul with regard to the organization of my material. When I was putting together the chapters for my book, Heaven is Here, I was inspired to write a chapter about spiritual Love – not ego Love, which is conditional. Immediately, I was shown a dodecahedron on my mental screen and was infused with the concept of becoming clear on what the aspects of spiritual Love are. I was then shown that there are twelve tangible aspects of spiritual Love.

This is because the dodecahedron represents ether or higher consciousness in Metatron's Cube – a sacred geometrical building block of all creation. Each of the five platonic solids contained therein are necessary for co-creation and the full function of the dodecahedron had been removed from the spiritual nomenclature during the fall of humanity on earth. Without Love (God) there cannot be creation.

Everything in our Universe is vibrational and electro magnetic in nature. These electrical fields contain information that is so miniscule and complex that our dense physical bodies and brains cannot comprehend what is contained therein. Yet, the information is vital to the creative force. While we are capable of genius beyond our comprehension, we are not equipped to understand the quantum level of physics (or smaller yet) that contains the information contained in the DNA of each cell that tells a flower cell to be a flower and a stomach cell to be a stomach. Even the most eloquent linguist or practiced channel cannot explain this.

Being multi-dimensional and complex, humankind has searched forever for the keys to salvation – the meaning of life – the Holy Grail. Our striving causes us to continually increase our ability to tap into the creative source and the meaning of life but we can only do so through symbolism, faith and intuition. (At this point in time) In the truest sense, Love is a powerful force that has no description. We may only hope to tap into it. Its power is beyond our comprehension or reasonable understanding. However, if we trust in it, we will experience the magic.

Embodying Christ Consciousness or unconditional Love is the most significant pathway to meshing with the vibration of Heaven on Earth.

What came through next made perfectly good sense to me. We as spiritualists and spiritual seekers speak of Love and we know it is within us, yet we often find ourselves loosing track of that place or alignment. It would be wise to grasp what it really is instead of haphazardly teetering between two worlds. By becoming the embodiment of Love, we become co-creators – extensions of God. This is what Christ did and this is what Christ taught. That is why he said, "Very truly I tell you, whoever believes in me will do the works I have been doing, and they will do even greater things than these, because I am."

These aspects are important for us as humans because we are spiritual beings working on blending our essence with the physical world. It has been said that this physical dimension is perhaps the most difficult for that reason. We as humans are very limited; yet capable of creating the energetic alignment we need in order to be receptors of this powerful creative force. We are only able to dispense and behold a limited volume of this powerful force, yet its embodiment and good works/will is why we are here.

I will be clarifying the meaning of Love in a spiritual sense. When we love a piece of cake or love a movie, we are actually talking about desire. Things such as desire, admiration, possession, passion, etc. are words that we use to describe ego-driven love. There is nothing wrong with loving these things – it is part of what we came here for – to enjoy all of the dimensions of being. When we love things of this Earth, we must also be prepared to let go because nothing here is permanent.

The only problem is these things will not bring inner peace because they are temporal. They merely enhance our enjoyment. The great thing about aligning with spiritual Love is that it is eternal. Love is meant to be our anchor. The more we exercise our spiritual muscles, the greater our spiritual power becomes and the larger our causal body becomes. The part of us that loves will never cease to be, though our body is part of the temporal world.

Here are the twelve main aspects of spiritual Love as I was given them. Most of them are in *A Course in Miracles – Manual for Teachers.* The aspects of Love that are in ACIM are:

Trust, Tolerance, Gentleness, Joy, Defenselessness, Generosity, Honesty, Patience, Faithfulness, Open-Mindedness

The other two aspects that I was given were *Appreciation* and *Expansiveness.*

You will find many of these characteristics or disciplines in esoteric teachings and most of them are in *A Course in Miracles.* If you are interested, ACIM is an Ascension manual that some people embrace and some people have difficulty with. I find that I cannot help but refer to it on a regular basis because it was so life confirming for me. Some may have trouble with the wording because there are subtleties in language that are not always obvious and not everybody hears things the same way. The variances in language lie in the subtle, unspoken content beyond the words and the way in which words are grouped. That is why things often have to be put in many different ways. It is not that one or the other is correct; it is that we all have different ways of understanding things.

After the descriptions of the aspects of Love, I will be discussing how the laws of metaphysics direct us in our search for higher ground. I have never cared for attempts

Christ Consciousness 77

to explain *A Course in Miracles* because it is a book that is meant to undo the ego, not a book that is meant to tell us what to do or drive conclusions. It is meant to return us in a place where the answers are self-evident. Because everything is subject to interpretation, it is best for people who want to study ACIM to keep his or her studying between his or her self and God. It is not wise to get other egos in the mix. In addition to this, healing requires that each person do the necessary soul searching and practice to integrate spiritual practices into his or her life. This is not something that another being can do for another.

Since I am including a substantial excerpt from ACIM, I thought I should give you an idea of what it is about, in case you are not familiar with the work. I will begin their inclusion in this booklet by including the introduction to ACIM, which I find to be immensely beautiful:

"This is a course in miracles. It is a required course. Only the time you take it is voluntary. Free will does not mean that you can establish the curriculum. It means only that you can elect what you want to take at a given time. The course does not aim at teaching the meaning of love, for that is beyond what can be taught. It does aim, however, at removing the blocks to the awareness of love's presence, which is your natural inheritance. The opposite of love is fear, but what is all encompassing can have no opposite."

This course can therefore be summed up very simply in this way:

Nothing real can be threatened.
Nothing unreal exists.
Herein lies the peace of God.

I especially like the references to real and unreal because it gives us permission to withdraw our attention to that which is not created by God. In time you must understand the fact that we get more of that which we focus on. Go ahead – embrace all that is good and kick everything else to the curb. We can really use this advice – especially now.

ACIM sums up the lengthy text by describing the characteristics of God's teachers. Even if we feel in our hearts that we are pure beings (and we should feel this way), we need to honestly examine ourselves on a daily basis to see where we may have developed contrary imprinting. We go through a re-mastering of the higher levels of consciousness in each lifetime, even if we Ascended in past lives or have come here from higher dimensions. This list and descriptions was very useful to me during the time when I re-Ascended my being in the early 1990's.

Here are the characteristics of God's teachers, as described in ACIM, which are also ten of the aspects of spiritual Love. You will find that everything that challenges you every day of your life can be compared to one of these traits for correction and clearing. I suggest that you read through the attributes and take in the magical nature of their descriptions. Notice where you may have resistance and work on the areas that you have difficulty with. It will take time to learn to assimilate them however.

Christ Consciousness

(Beginning of ACIM Excerpt)

The surface traits of God's teachers are not at all alike. They do not look alike to the body's eyes, they come from vastly different backgrounds, their experiences of the world vary greatly, and their superficial "personalities" are quite distinct. Nor, at the beginning stages of their functioning as teachers of God, have they as yet acquired the deeper characteristics that will establish them as what they are. God gives special gifts to His teachers, because they have a special role in His plan for Atonement. Their specialness is, of course, only temporary; set in time as a means of leading out of time. These special gifts, born in the holy relationship toward which the teaching-learning situation is geared, become characteristic of all teachers of God who have advanced in their own learning. In this respect they are all alike.

All differences among the Sons of God are temporary. Nevertheless, in time it can be said that the advanced teachers of God have the following characteristics:

Trust

This is the foundation on which their ability to fulfill their function rests. Perception is the result of learning. In fact, perception is learning, because cause and effect are never separated. The teachers of God have trust in the world, because they have learned it is not governed by the laws the world made up. It is governed by a power that is in them but not of them. It is this power that keeps all things safe. It is through this power that the teachers of God look on a forgiven world.

When this power has once been experienced, it is impossible to trust one's own petty strength again. Who would attempt to fly with the tiny wings of a sparrow when the mighty power of an eagle has been given him? And who would place his faith in the shabby offerings of the ego when the gifts of God are laid before him? What is it that induces them to make the shift?

First, they must go through what might be called "a period of undoing." This need not be painful, but it usually is so experienced. It seems as if things are being taken away, and it is rarely understood initially that their lack of value is merely being recognized. How can lack of value be perceived unless the perceiver is in a position where he must see things in a different light? He is not yet at a point at which he can make the shift entirely internally. And so the plan will sometimes call for changes in what seem to be external circumstances. These changes are always helpful. When the teacher of God has learned that much, he goes on to the second stage.

Next, the teacher of God must go through "a period of sorting out." This is always somewhat difficult because, having learned that the changes in his life are always helpful, he must now decide all things on the basis of whether they increase the helpfulness or hamper it. He will find that many, if not most of the things he valued before will merely hinder his ability to transfer what he has learned to new situations as they arise. Because he has valued what is really valueless, he will not generalize the lesson for fear of loss and sacrifice. It takes great learning to understand that all things, events, encounters and circumstances are helpful. It is only to the extent to which they are helpful that any degree of reality should be accorded them in this world of illusion. The word "value" can apply to nothing else.

The third stage through which the teacher of God must go can be called "a period of relinquishment." If this is interpreted as giving up the desirable, it will engender enormous conflict. Few teachers of God escape this distress entirely. There is, however, no point in sorting out the valuable from the valueless unless the next obvious step is taken. Therefore, the period of overlap is apt to be one in which the teacher of God feels called upon to sacrifice his own best interests on behalf of truth. He has not realized as yet how wholly impossible such a demand would be. He can learn this only as he actually does give up the valueless. Through this, he learns that where he anticipated grief, he finds a happy lightheartedness instead; where he thought something was asked of him, he finds a gift bestowed on him. Now comes "a period of settling down." This is a quiet time, in which the teacher of God rests a while in reasonable peace. Now he consolidates his learning. Now he begins to see the transfer value of what he has learned. Its potential is literally staggering, and the teacher of God is now at the point in his progress at which he sees in it his whole way out. "Give up what you do not want, and keep what you do." How simple is the obvious! And how easy to do! The teacher of God needs this period of respite. He has not yet come as far as he thinks. Yet when he is ready to go on, he goes with mighty companions beside him. Now he rests a while, and gathers them before going on. He will not go on from here alone.

The next stage is indeed "a period of unsettling." Now must the teacher of God understand that he did not really know what was valuable and what was valueless. All that he really learned so far was that he did not want the valueless, and that he did want the valuable. Yet his own sorting out was meaningless in teaching him the difference. The idea of sacrifice, so central to his own thought system, had made it impossible for him to judge. He thought he learned willingness, but now he sees that he does not know what the willingness is for. And now he must attain a state that may remain impossible to reach for a long, long time. He must learn to lay all judgment aside, and ask only what he really wants in every circumstance. Were not each step in this direction so heavily reinforced, it would be hard indeed!

And finally, there is "a period of achievement." It is here that learning is consolidated. Now what was seen as merely shadows before become solid gains, to be counted on in all "emergencies" as well as tranquil times. Indeed, the tranquility is their result; the outcome of honest learning, consistency of thought and full transfer. This is the stage of real peace, for here is Heaven's state fully reflected. From here, the way to Heaven is open and easy. In fact, it is here. Who would "go" anywhere, if peace of mind is already complete? And who would seek to change tranquility for something more desirable? What could be more desirable than this?

Honesty

All other traits of God's teachers rest on trust. Once that has been achieved, the others cannot fail to follow. Only the trusting can afford honesty, for only they can see its value. Honesty does not apply only to what you say. The term actually means consistency. There is nothing you say that contradicts what you think or do; no thought opposes any other thought; no act belies your word; and no word lacks agreement with another. Such are the truly honest. At no level are they in conflict with themselves. Therefore it is impossible for them to be in conflict with anyone or anything.

The peace of mind which the advanced teachers of God experience is largely due to their perfect honesty. It is only the wish to deceive that makes for war. No one at one with himself can even conceive of conflict. Conflict is the inevitable result of self-deception, and self-deception is dishonesty. There is no challenge to a teacher of God. Challenge implies doubt, and the trust on which God's teachers rest secure makes doubt impossible. Therefore they can only succeed. In this, as in all things, they are honest. They can only succeed, because they never do their will alone. They choose for all mankind; for all the world and all things in it; for the unchanging and unchangeable beyond appearances; and for the Son of God and his Creator. How could they not succeed? They choose in perfect honesty, sure of their choice as of themselves.

Tolerance

God's teachers do not judge. To judge is to be dishonest, for to judge is to assume a position you do not have. Judgment without self-deception is impossible. Judgment implies that you have been deceived in your brothers. How, then, could you not have been deceived in yourself? Judgment implies a lack of trust, and trust remains the bedrock of the teacher of God's whole thought system. Let this be lost, and all his learning goes. Without judgment are all things equally acceptable, for who could judge otherwise? Without judgment are all men brothers, for who is there who stands apart? Judgment destroys honesty and shatters trust. No teacher of God can judge and hope to learn.

Gentleness

Harm is impossible for God's teachers. They can neither harm nor be harmed. Harm is the outcome of judgment. It is the dishonest act that follows a dishonest thought. It is a verdict of guilt upon a brother, and therefore on oneself. It is the end of peace and the denial of learning. It demonstrates the absence of God's curriculum, and its replacement by insanity. No teacher of God but must learn,--and fairly early in his training,-- that harmfulness completely obliterates his function from his awareness. It will make him confused, fearful, angry and suspicious. It will make the Holy Spirit's lessons impossible to learn. Nor can God's Teacher be heard at all, except by those who realize that harm can actually achieve nothing. No gain can come of it. Therefore, God's teachers are wholly gentle. They need the strength of gentleness, for it is in this that the function of salvation becomes easy. To those who would do harm, it is impossible. To those to whom harm has no meaning, it is merely natural. What choice but this has meaning to the sane? Who chooses hell when he perceives a way to Heaven? And who would choose the weakness that must come from harm in place of the unfailing, all- encompassing and limitless strength of gentleness? The might of God's teachers lies in their gentleness, for they have understood their evil thoughts came neither from God's Son nor his Creator. Thus did they join their thoughts with Him Who is their

Source. And so their will, which always was His Own, is free to be itself.

Joy

Joy is the inevitable result of gentleness. Gentleness means that fear is now impossible, and what could come to interfere with joy? The open hands of gentleness are always filled. The gentle have no pain. They cannot suffer. Why would they not be joyous? They are sure they are beloved and must be safe. Joy goes with gentleness as surely as grief attends attack. God's teachers trust in Him. And they are sure His Teacher goes before them, making sure no harm can come to them. They hold His gifts and follow in His way, because God's Voice directs them in all things. Joy is their song of thanks. And Christ looks down on them in thanks as well. His need of them is just as great as theirs of Him. How joyous it is to share the purpose of salvation!

Defenselessness

God's teachers have learned how to be simple. They have no dreams that need defense against the truth. They do not try to make themselves. Their joy comes from their understanding Who created them. And does what God created need defense? No one can become an advanced teacher of God until he fully understands that defenses are but foolish guardians of mad illusions. The more grotesque the dream, the fiercer and more powerful its defenses seem to be. Yet when the teacher of God finally agrees to look past them, he finds that nothing was there. Slowly at first he lets himself be undeceived. But he learns faster as his trust increases. It is not danger that comes when defenses are laid down. It is safety. It is peace. It is joy. And it is God.

Generosity

The term generosity has special meaning to the teacher of God. It is not the usual meaning of the word; in fact, it is a meaning that must be learned and learned very carefully. Like all the other attributes of God's teachers this one rests ultimately on trust, for without trust no one can be generous in the true sense. To the world, generosity means "giving away" in the sense of "giving up." To the teachers of God, it means giving away in order to keep. This has been emphasized throughout the text and the workbook, but it is perhaps more alien to the thinking of the world than many other ideas in our curriculum. Its greater strangeness lies merely in the obviousness of its reversal of the world's thinking. In the clearest way possible, and at the simplest of levels, the word means the exact opposite to the teachers of God and to the world. The teacher of God is generous out of Self interest. This does not refer, however, to the self of which the world speaks. The teacher of God does not want anything he cannot give away, because he realizes it would be valueless to him by definition. What would he want it for? He could only lose because of it. He could not gain. Therefore he does not seek what only he could keep, because that is a guarantee of loss. He does not want to suffer. Why should he ensure himself pain? But he does want to keep for himself all things that are of God, and therefore for His Son. These are the things that belong to him. These he can give away in true generosity, protecting them forever for himself.

Patience

Those who are certain of the outcome can afford to wait, and wait without anxiety. Patience is natural to the teacher of God. All he sees is certain outcome, at a time perhaps unknown to him as yet, but not in doubt. The time will be as right as is the answer. And this is true for everything that happens now or in the future. The past as well held no mistakes; nothing that did not serve to benefit the world, as well as him to whom it seemed to happen. Perhaps it was not understood at the time. Even so, the teacher of God is willing to reconsider all his past decisions, if they are causing pain to anyone. Patience is natural to those who trust. Sure of the ultimate interpretation of all things in time, no outcome already seen or yet to come can cause them fear.

Faithfulness

The extent of the teacher of God's faithfulness is the measure of his advancement in the curriculum. Does he still select some aspects of his life to bring to his learning, while keeping others apart? If so, his advancement is limited, and his trust not yet firmly established. Faithfulness is the teacher of God's trust in the Word of God to set all things right; not some, but all. Generally, his faithfulness begins by resting on just some problems, remaining carefully limited for a time. To give up all problems to one Answer is to reverse the thinking of the world entirely. And that alone is faithfulness. Nothing but that really deserves the name. Yet each degree, however small, is worth achieving. Readiness, as the text notes, is not mastery.

True faithfulness, however, does not deviate. Being consistent, it is wholly honest. Being unswerving, it is full of trust. Being based on fearlessness, it is gentle. Being certain, it is joyous. And being confident, it is tolerant. Faithfulness, then, combines in itself the other attributes of God's teachers. It implies acceptance of the Word of God and His definition of His Son. It is to Them that faithfulness in the true sense is always directed. Toward Them it looks, seeking until it finds. Defenselessness attends it naturally, and joy is its condition. And having found, it rests in quiet certainty on that alone to which all faithfulness is due.

Open-Mindedness

The centrality of open-mindedness, perhaps the last of the attributes the teacher of God acquires, is easily understood when its relation to forgiveness is recognized. Open-mindedness comes with lack of judgment. As judgment shuts the mind against God's Teacher, so open-mindedness invites Him to come in. As condemnation judges the Son of God as evil, so open-mindedness permits him to be judged by the Voice for God on His behalf. As the projection of guilt upon him would send him to hell, so open- mindedness lets Christ's image be extended to him. Only the open-minded can be at peace, for they alone see reason for it.

How do the open-minded forgive? They have let go all things that would prevent forgiveness. They have in truth abandoned the world, and let it be restored to them in newness and in joy so glorious they could never have conceived of such a change. Nothing is now as it was formerly. Nothing but sparkles now which seemed so dull and lifeless before. And above all are all things welcoming, for threat is gone. No clouds remain to hide the face of Christ. Now is the goal achieved. Forgiveness is the final goal of the curriculum. It paves the way for what goes far beyond all learning. The curriculum makes no effort to exceed its legitimate goal. Forgiveness is its single aim, at which all learning ultimately converges. It is indeed enough. **(End of ACIM excerpt)**

As for the two additional traits that I was given by spirit:

Appreciation is the doorway that provides for reciprocating energy flow – the constant give and take that provides for constant nourishment; the breathing in and the breathing out of spirit. It acknowledges the interdependent nature of our existence and the appreciation for the interdependent cooperation.

Expansiveness is the willingness and ability to allow one's self to continually be open to Source and grow in light, depth and understanding without reprieve.
We have this spark of Love in us that we have not been taught to nurture – yet we would not be alive without it. If we use it and nurture it, it expands and increases in the power to heal. When we come to the point where we have heightened the power of the spirit within, we are grounded, content and at peace with everything. Whenever we find ourselves misaligned with peace, it means we need to stop and observe what caused us to lose our footing. This is how we re-program ourselves to operate from a different perspective.

So here it is, in its least complicated form, the Ascension ladder, leading to attainment of higher levels of consciousness merely requires us to embrace the concept of spiritual Love. All of this exists inside of us, so it is a matter of clearing out the blockages to Love's awareness. As we integrate the aspects of spiritual Love into all of our being, we then transform everything in our path. Once we are attuned with the higher frequencies, we are in sync with creation itself.

The Ascension process is a solo journey. It is an endeavor of tremendous self-responsibility. It is not possible to coerce another person to take the journey, nor is it possible to be responsible for another person's journey. We may however, positively affect someone else's journey as well as the evolution of the planet if we are vibrating high enough to bring divine energy into the physical realm. All other energies are dust to dust and have little or no power.

Ascension not only involves purification of the heart, it involves purification and harmonization of all of our bodies. As a unit of consciousness, we exist in many different levels and ideally we harmonize them and balance them for optimum benefit. While I have mentioned that it is critical at this juncture in human evolution to gain a stronger connection to our soul, it is not all we need to refine and nurture. We need to take excellent care of our physical bodies and brains and work to have all of our parts working together in harmony.

It is wise to align our desires with the desires of our soul even if logic tells us otherwise.

The demands of modern society cause us to be so busy paying the bills and entertaining ourselves that we don't even take care of our bodies properly and we do not hear the still small voice inside of our feeling center. We eat quick and easy food, which is not always good for us, and we don't give our bodies and minds time to rejuvenate. When our system fails us, we take pills. As a consequence, we deplete the natural resources that are there to sustain life. Instead of running on spiritual power, we run on energy drinks and adrenalin. This is why we glamorize violence, male dominated sexual images and competition - we crave the adrenalin and testosterone rushes that come along with them. We don't get rid of the drug dealer; we get rid of the need for the drug.

An important part of the Ascension process is making it a priority to slow down and live a mindful life – becoming aware of the subtle impulses and instincts we have developed or are picking up from the cacophony. Furthermore, when we live mindfully, we begin the process of reconnecting and it takes time to get used to this state. We are so accustomed to living outside of our self. We start the inner journey slowly and practice getting stronger in our connection every day. I have heard this referred to as the thousand-day climb. We may only do so much in a day. Patterns take time to change and integrate.

When we expand our connection to Source energy or Love, we enjoy an increasingly more intense natural high instead.

Atonement begins with surrendering to our soul...

This can be done right where you stand and it doesn't cost anything. You will however, need to do a great deal of clearing work and spend gloriously long periods of time with your soul before you are securely anchored into a new paradigm. Some may feel they are stuck because of financial or relationship responsibilities. There are ways to cope with these issues, and each individual needs to work things out in their own way. There is a solution to every problem but solutions are very specific to individual situations.

If you don't feel you have enough money to take time away from responsibilities, do your best to make sure you spend at least a little time being still every day. Have quiet places to go, especially in nature. Remember that you get more of what you focus on, so if you demonstrate to the Universe that you demand down time, you will eventually get more of it!

Once the decision to reach higher ground is made, an energetic alignment is spurred and then the rest of the process falls into place. One thing that is not often mentioned is that there is a process that one goes through when they rise. We cannot force the process or skip things. We surrender and accept etheric help to keep the process on track.

Think of Ascension as untying a tangled rope or unscrambling a Rubik's cube. The wisdom of the creative force knows that one thing has to occur before another and sometimes a move has to be made that appears to be backwards, yet it is a necessary step that needs to occur before the next. This is why we have to step back and become the observer. Let the energy show you what is being highlighted every day. This is what ACIM means by the "curriculum." You will be amazed by the hidden wisdom of creation.

You will likely have one day that presents you with challenges followed by one day of rest and integration.

The great part about the process is that you don't have to decide what's next. The wisdom of the energy knows how to highlight and transmute. Karmic relationships may be highlighted for a period of time. People may come back into your life for review. Difficult situations will pop up. Surrender to the process and handle everything that appears to your highest ability.

Handling what comes your way is what you do to clear the karma of the physical. At the same time, the spiritual muscles need to be built. This is achieved by spending time alone and spending time in a still space, whether active or contemplative. The main thing is that one must listen to the guidance within and allow it to reveal itself. Once this connection is strong, it is yours to keep throughout eternity. It always was yours – you just lost track of it. Thank God for that!

If you are looking for a weekend fix, you have come to the wrong place. I have found that the return to Christ Consciousness is work, primarily because we have accumulated so much and we have buried so much in our psyches and our karmic debris fields that we don't even know what's in there. How do we begin to sort through what we find in the Pandora's box that is our karmic history?

At various intervals in your ascent, you will discover the missing pieces of your soul, your purpose, your life goals and perhaps some of the history thereof. Sometimes you will get stirrings around things that interested you when you were young and sometimes you may simply surprise your self. Make sure you take time to integrate new thoughts and feelings.

This is not a time to be seeking out of body experiences. This is a time to correct the path of our planet and our species. At this time, the people who are incarnated on Earth are either finishing up balancing their karma or they are people who have incarnated to help others. We need to have compassion and respect for each other. Moving into the fifth dimension and cleaning up the debris from the third dimension is what we are doing right now. We can explore about other dimensions when we finish our work in the few dimensions that we need to function well here.

Because Ascension is a solo journey, there is a good chance you will find your self moving away from the crowds you are accustomed to running with, unless they are working on Ascension as well. Truthfully, I find that many people are trying hard to hang on to what they are familiar and comfortable with, rather that getting a little lighter, clearer and more expansive every day. Just as the river flows and the tree grows toward the sky, humans are also designed to reach higher and higher ground. The people who are stuck will move when they are ready and not because you want them to. Eventually the ego tires and surrenders to spirit.

Getting back to the process of climbing the spiral…
As we evolve, we carry information with us from lifetime to lifetime. The wisdom and knowledge that we gained

in each life follows us and is available in our chakra system. This is why some famous musicians who were child protégées were able to pick up their instruments and play at such a young age. Itzak Pearlman, Akim Camera and Yo-yo Ma are examples of this level of genius. As we gain wisdom, this too is stored in our chakras and this is why it is important to keep them clear and operating properly in order to live successfully and authentically.

For self-healing, notice when an uncomfortable thought or feeling arises and slow down enough to detect where you are feeling it in your body. Each area of our body represents karmic patterning. Study up on the meaning of the chakras to determine where your biggest problems lie.

Becoming aware of our triggers and discordant energy patterns is the first step in the Ascension process. You see, when the things of our lives come up, we are meant to handle them in such a way that they create higher wisdom for us. All too often, we don't gain higher wisdom and we just stuff our feelings down and that is how the misinformation gets lodged in our chakras. This is how we become jaded, wounded, negative and sluggish. We react to new situations with garbled messages when our chakras are not clear. We can regain our energy and our health by healing those chakras by re-visiting the things in our lives that we did not handle properly (for the highest good) when they occurred. Some of us may have many, many events that we need to heal.

If we attempt to release our processing and perception to our greater self and there is not a sense of relief or opening, then we need to see what the reasons are. Remembering always to be very patient and gentle with your self throughout the process, try to find the thing that is tying you up the most. Is it fear of the unknown? Is it a relationship or something your parents projected on you? I have heard that our image of God is actually a projection of our parent's imprinting. This is a concept most of us have not really thought about. I think that this is a very good exercise to begin your ascent with. It is a good idea to know where you are headed and what your destination is before you embark on a journey. Let's make sure the vision is accurate and positive before you begin.

The process of healing the self is the atonement – the return to innocence.

What good will it do for one person to move into higher consciousness, while others struggle and act out? Quantum level energy and beyond has its own sets of laws that guide the physics therein. Everything is programmed to reach ever-increasing vibrations. Anything that is not co-created with Source or quantum energy, does not have staying power, or any real power at all for that matter. Comfort lies in knowing that any higher energies that are co-mingled into the lower, denser energies, will eradicate the those lower energies in time. Higher energies are like spiritual solvent or cosmic Drano. Higher vibrations trump lower vibrations. Therefore, one person, having obtained the state of Ascension on Earth, will cause all matter to eventually succumb to the higher states. When Christ Jesus accomplished Ascension, his gift was left in Earth's vibratory field.

When you hear that Christ Jesus saved us by rising from

the dead - this is what it means. Another way of looking at it is that Christ showed us that it was possible. In order to align, we must also rise above the difficulty of the density of the lower planes of existence.

It is the fault of nothing save our own ego identification that we lose our way. We all come in with things to resolve - things to do - karma to reverse, etc. We choose parents and circumstances that will highlight all of those things we need to make us better eternal beings. All of the difficulties are blessings in disguise - revealing their benefits most often after we surrender to them and stop judging them. We also tend to reincarnate with the same people over and over. It can get pretty gluey and sludgy. I recommend that you bypass hashing it out with all the people who wronged you. I do recommend apologizing to those you have wronged. This is starting to sound like a twelve step program. The guy who developed the twelve-step program believed that he received the guidance for the system from his higher self. I am sure he did. Anyway, Ascension requires that we take TOTAL responsibility for our atonement or return to innocence.

We must want Ascension more than we want justice. Each person who chooses the path of Ascension takes countless and unknown others with them energetically through quantum entanglement.

We must be very forgiving and compassionate at this time. Everybody is going to have his or her own way of moving into the higher energies. Some people may just make a decision to live with their heart and as long as they keep re-aligning, all will be well. Others may have some severe traumas to work through and heal. Still others have years and years of programming in their minds and in their energy that needs to be trained away.

Learning how to be introspective and seek help from the higher realms will be the norm for humans for quite some time. While we were being trained to be good factory workers in the last couple centuries, we now must learn how to be good co-creators. We need to be able to chisel out time every day, or every time we feel as though we are stuck or not coping. We must give ourselves permission to take that time and prioritize our spiritual growth. It needs to be part of our routine, just like shopping, eating, going to work, etc.

Some people will be good at locating their difficulties and healing the discordant energy. There are those who will need help from others. I suggest finding a good intuitive guide to help you when you get stuck and develop a strong relationship with your inner guidance. Learn how to ask a question of the Universe learn to hear the answer. It is necessary to be as neutral as possible in order to receive information. Answers may come from anywhere and at any time.

Be careful when you ask for wisdom or answers to intend that Christ, Archangel Michael, Mother Mary, or any other healing Angels or Masters be present. Deceased relatives or seeming spirit guides may or may not be the best sources of information and if you are not properly trained, you may be tricked by lower vibrating beings.
We can only see in others, that which we see in ourselves. When we see our own innocence, we then see the innocence in others. When we see our brilliance, we see the brilliance in others. Why do we need to see all

Christ Consciousness

this magnificence? We need to see it because it IS the truth of who we really are and the negativity and heaviness is NOT the truth of who we are. If we are not seeing things in a more positive light, then we are functioning on false pretenses. We have suffered long enough by being separated from our spirits and the suffering can now be over. The darkness has brainwashed us into thinking that life has to be hard and that is simply not the truth.

It is time to re-program. If we cannot succeed in re-connecting with our God-selves, our species could be harmed once again, but I don't believe it is going to happen. Intuition tells me that enough people are going to achieve alignment to save the planet.

Before we pursue other goals, let us first have peace on Earth and learn to live harmoniously as the magnificent beings that we were meant to be. That is why we are here and it is our priority at this time. This is why the world you see appears to be falling apart. Let it fall. We have to create new pathways. When you look upon all the things in the news and when you are challenged by the individual circumstances of your life, know that you always have the choice to create something new and that it only takes one person to make a difference. You never know how many people will hear your voice and come out of the closet to join you.

Understanding that our soul never leaves us and that it is always there to lead us is a great treasure and comfort. It is our anchor in these tumultuous times. I consider a connection to this energy to be at the only way to feel really rooted and strong. When and if the world spins into even greater chaos, a connection to your soul will

stabilize you and guide you.
To know one's self is to know Heaven. The greatest thing we may accomplish and the greatest gift we could give the world is to strip away the karmic debris and become the embodiment of our authentic self.

When we align our desires with the goals of our soul, we are in Heaven – we are in an Ascended state.
THIS my friends is the Holy Grail.

All quotes from A Course in Miracles are from the Second Edition, 1996, ©Foundation for Inner Peace, P.O. Box 598, Mill Valley, 94942-0598, www.acim.org and info@acim.org.

Recommended Reading:

A Course in Miracles - Foundation for Inner Peace

Bonus Material: Meditation Made Simple

Meditation is a state of mind where we have allowed the brain to slow down to the level of theta and we have also brought our consciousness to our center. The Latin root of medi is middle. The words meditate and medium come to mind as these are words we use to describe someone who is bridging the spiritual and the physical by being aware of both of them at the same time. They have achieved a state of being in the middle or in between. In time many people will all come to value this optimal positioning. This position, when embraced by many will restore our planet to a state of Heaven on Earth because this is in essence what we are doing when we bridge the two planes. You have heard the expression, as above, so below. This is how we bring the heavenly state into physical being.

Meditation is not an altered state, nor is it an escape or an out of body experience. Quite the contrary, we are designed to rest in the middle between higher and lower consciousness. This is the place that is often described as the vortex or the center and is the place where we bring higher intelligence into the physical world. This state may also be called the place of co-creation. Co-creation is the act of tapping into the vortex of creation and it is the place where all creative genius comes from. It is the place where we may bring into physical form, that which is received in a state of cooperative synergy between the physical and the spiritual sides of life.

Because of the fast paced, highly demanding environment most of us live in, we have trained ourselves to become overly focused on the physical. As I mentioned, we are really designed to straddle both worlds, but we have not been taught how to do this. Because many of us have exhausted ourselves by trying to live unilaterally, we are feeling the pull to experience the spiritual side of life.

What happens when our brain cycles are moving too quickly it gets caught up in its own frenetic conversation or story. Too much activity and the brain just makes us shut down or even worse, it makes us want to lash out at someone or something. The brain becomes useless when it is rushing too quickly and is not able to retrieve knowledge or stored information, including rational thought. Overuse on a continual basis will cause chronic mental fog and fatigue also.

What we experience in the world then, is a clashing of agendas. Conflict is the result of people getting caught up in the mind, experiencing rapid-fire impulses of a non-descript nature, colliding with others in the same state.

Imagine a world where everybody is in a much more relaxed, co-operative state of mind, centered in their divine instincts, taking advantage of co-creation and divine timing to move through their lives. When you meditate, not only do you benefit your mind and your body, you add to the good in the world by living in integrity. When we are in this space, we bring a high level of wisdom and peace to all situations.

The spiritual side of creation is life giving and always flowing. If we stay tapped into the vortex of creation, we can enjoy a much more fruitful and healthy life. I believe that once we learn how to be in a meditative state, we can learn how to live with our lives fully anchored in both spheres of consciousness. The theta brain wave state is optimal for synching your instincts and actions and can be maintained throughout all of your waking hours. When the brain cycles are slowed down, they move slowly through the mass of information that is stored in our brain and operate in the proper mode for the co-creative state.

In the meantime, I suggest that you set aside one half hour, two times a day to become accustomed to the meditative state. Once you become comfortable with it, you may start to integrate it into your daily life. All the while being careful to make sure that you have your feet solidly planted on the ground, the things of life will initially seem like a beautiful dream. This is because you have aligned with a different perspective that has been there all along, yet you were not aware of it.

Until you are able to return to a more peaceful state of mind with great ease, I suggest that you prepare your self for meditation. Start by putting on some peaceful music. You definitely want to set aside everything you think you may need to worry about. You could write all of the things that you are toiling over on a piece of paper. This gives the mind the feeling that it is still keeping track of everything, while letting go of it for a period of time. If you have other ways of letting go of issues, please go ahead and use them. Either way, I suggest you prepare yourself by winding down and letting go gradually. When you feel like you are ready, it is time to let go of the outer world and join with your inner world, which has always been there and always will be. While you are focusing on your center, you will still hear the outer world, but it will not take your full attention off of the inner space.

When we meditate or move into a state of balance between the outer and inner worlds, we have to intentionally slow down our brain cycles. This begins to happen as soon as we focus on our center. Our center is literally in the center of our physical body. Our center of being is accessed through focusing on the breath. Our breath is the physical manifestation of our soul and it rests in our feeling center, which lies between the solar plexus chakra around our belly and goes up to our throat chakra. It is desirable to feel your breath fill this whole area as though it is a big vessel.

If you find yourself wanting to go to sleep when you slow down, I suggest that you trust yourself and allow yourself to go to sleep. Hopefully, you will only take a brief power nap, after which you may resume your work on balancing the spheres. Perhaps your brain was over-worked and needed a rest first.

Otherwise, simply focus on your gentle breathing and feel the life-giving nature of this practice. You are filling up your feeling center and clearing out the clutter. With each gentle cleansing breath, you are becoming more aligned with your soul. I don't feel that there is a specific way to sit or a specific way to breath. Just make it comfortable and make it gentle. As you move deeper into your meditative state, you should feel the heaviness and cacophony of your head diminishing and you should begin to feel the glow and warmth of your inner space.

It is important that you don't expect anything to happen while you do this. As soon as you expect something, you have interfered with the process of alignment. At best, in the early stages of learning to slow down, you should expect nothing but to feel bathed in the energy of your inner light. As a matter of fact, until you are practiced at this you will probably not have any big epiphanies. This is perfectly OK. You will, however, benefit from the rest you are giving your brain as well as the receiving of high vibrating energy through your feeling center.

When you first begin to slow down your mental processing, your brain is able to re-arrange itself and reprogram the way it functions. It is programmed to organize and de-clutter, so as long as we don't interfere by over-using it, the new normal will set in over time. In time you will develop a genius brain that is very well organized and has great retrieval and storage function.

Not only is the practice of meditation a life-changing practice, it is a great way to recharge during the day.

You may contact Alana Kay at Alana@alanakay.com or visit Ms. Kay's website: www.alanakay.com

Other books and booklets by Alana Kay:

How to Give & Receive a Quality Intuitive Reading (booklet – ebook only)

Heaven is Here, Our Ascent into the Fifth Dimension

Ascension Through the Twelve Aspects of Christ Consciousness

Wishing On Your Own Star

The 12 Aspects of Love Meditation CD

About the Author

Having grown up in a typical American family, I have struggled all of my life to blend the very esoteric me in to a world of form where everything I am seems to be going against the grain. The pull to be myself has always been stronger than the pull to be like the crowd, yet I have consistently remained enmeshed with the people and structures of modern society, closely observing and constantly playing with the dynamics and the energy – trying to find ways to make it palatable – a state which some refer to as, being in the world, but not of it.

I have had my ancient eyes open since I can remember, but have had to be patient while more has been gradually revealed to me over time as I have moved through challenges and deepened the connection to my soul.

I am about to describe many of the hardships and challenges I encountered in my growing years because I know that most people have to deal with a great deal more than most of us realize.

From a very young age, I was already aware that I was an intuitive medium. All people who are sensitives or energetics are aware of this fact early in life because they are visited by spirits, are very sensitive to energies of all types and are hyper-aware of human behavior on a deep or spiritual level.

I spent countless hours awake every night trying to hide from the spirits that appeared in the night and alternatively spent many hours contemplating the deeper meaning of life until the wee hours of the morning. I often heard words of wisdom that seemed to be coming from a being that was resonating with my own being. I have since come to understand the complex metaphysical phenomenon that manifests as this wise resonance. It is the field of Christ Consciousness and my soul is connected to it through quantum entanglement.

Because everything is electromagnetic and connected through quantum entanglement, the higher realms of consciousness became available to me when the world was quiet and my mind was still. Because I always felt close to Christ Jesus, I believed this resonance to be him, although it was actually Christ Consciousness - the realm where ascended beings exist. This realm is omnipresent because it is of the highest vibration.

Because I was open and sensitive, I was also taunted by lesser spirits as well. When I was younger, I dreaded the night. By learning to receive answers from the masters, create filters and keep a consistently high vibration, I no longer dread the dark or the night; I sleep very well as a matter of fact. I did have to work on things and it required a commitment and investment of time.

I was gangly, skinny, knock-kneed and shy and felt very awkward in my earlier years. I spent the first couple years of my life in leg braces because my hip joints were severely out of alignment. My family was poorer than most and my clothes were hand-me-downs. All of this made me feel very self-conscious and the children who were my peers made it painfully obvious that I was indeed awkward and different. I was picked on and told by my mother to turn the other cheek, which made me feel as though I should not defend myself. The things we are told when we are young become our programming because it is all we know when we are new to the world.

Everything about me made me feel like an outsider and I was very disempowered. The home I grew up in was full of stress. I suffered headaches from a young age and always felt agitated and physically and mentally uncomfortable. I fought short bouts of depression and was an insomniac until I set out on my own at age 18, when I was more able to be my true self and be more free.

Given that I had a very spiritual bent from the beginning of life, growing up surrounded by an atheistic family was one of the first challenges I remember having to deal with. As the family member who felt all the pain, I was subject to outbursts because all of the stress and pain was internalized by me. Because of this and because I was different, I was labeled the black sheep - a projection that took me many years to correct in my own mind. Since most families seem to have a black sheep - the one who challenges everybody's reality - one has to wonder if this is part of a divine plan.

Many older souls become alcoholics and drug addicts, depending on the level of dysfunction that the given family suffers. I escaped the path of the addict, even though many in my birth family are alcoholics.

In my earlier adult life, I attracted people who brought reenactment of my familial relationships. I discovered

To Know Thy Self Is to Know Heaven

Jesus said, "If those who lead you say to you,
'See, the kingdom is in heaven,'
Then the birds of heaven will precede you.
If they say to you,
'It is in the sea,'
Then the fish will precede you.
But the kingdom is inside of you.
And it is outside of you.
"When you become acquainted with yourselves,
then you will be recognized.
And you will understand that it is you who are
Children of the living father.
But if you do not become acquainted
With yourselves,
Then you are in poverty, and it is you
Who are the poverty."

as many other have, that all of my childhood memories were lodged in my holographic field and mental patterning, causing the drama to play out in my life over and over. Our past remains in our attractor field unless we clear it out.

My family relationships also played a role in my development of self-karma. I grew up with an undue amount of criticism and competition which fueled a belief that I needed to prove to the world as well as myself that I was OK. This made me over achiever and a perfectionist. Perfection was my way of making sure that I would not endure criticism or complaints, and this quest for perfection is forever elusive because it is not truly attainable in the physical world.

As a result, the world became a reflection of my own beliefs. The interesting thing was that the closer that I got to perfection with things, the more I found myself having to endure criticism! I was attracting other perfectionists – for whom nothing was ever good enough, regularly confirming my inner beliefs, so I had to constantly seek higher levels of perfection in the hope that one day everything would be up to par with my impossible standards. One way that I found to correct my perfectionism was to strive for excellence and let Spirit handle perfection.

This type of imbalance is very common in our human experience and with intuitive introspection and careful spiritual analysis, we can re-arrange all of our past patterning and past experiences the same way. All of the information from our history is in the Akashic records. Because of our soul history and innate personality, we all experience and assimilate things differently.

My extremely inquisitive nature, much like that of today's indigo and crystal children, resulted in a general disposition of boredom with everyday life, and still does to this day. Seeking solace and adventure, and as young as seven years old, I gravitated to the neighborhood churches whose doors were open to the public in 1960's. I felt a deep level of peace in these holy places and I felt a sense of belonging there that I did not feel at my family home.

I felt a connection to Spirit for the first time, standing alone in a Catholic church. Familiar but indescribable feelings of bliss, depth and contentment rose seemingly out of nowhere. The vigil candles flickering in the corner, the lingering scent of frankincense and myrrh, and the stillness and the stature took me to a place inside of me that was entirely different than the one that had been projected on me by my family and my peers. Swaddled inside these hallowed walls, I longed to be of service to God and often envisioned myself as a nun, priest or monk.

The thought of living a life of devotion to spiritual matters has always intrigued me. In reflection, this makes sense, since I have discovered through meditation that my soul history that of the Order of Melchezedek - an eternal priesthood. The Order of Melchezedek are souls that always dedicate their lives to the spiritual advancement of humanity and always incarnate to be of service.

In this lifetime, I have had to find ways of weaving my soul into normal every day circumstances. It is possible to do so, but requires a high degree of mastership. I am sure that in past lives I lived in monasteries and such, where living in connection to spirit was the norm. Spiritual pursuits, especially at this point in our evolution do not have to exist solely outside of the grind. I see the benefit of this and I hope everybody else does, because this is the time for all of us to bring our special offerings to the table of life. I see the day when corporate America embraces spiritual teachings to improve business.

Bits and pieces of information came in to me over the years and some of them have stood out in my memory. I had moments of epiphany that would yield small fruit and then be put on the shelf until a later date. There were not any existing avenues in my mind or in my environment that would support any further adventure. Although I usually felt it was par for the course, there have been many times when I felt trapped in this low vibrating society.

These days, there is so much available for the spiritual seeker. With the proliferation of spiritual literature and the Internet, no stone should remain unturned.

Beyond our fears lay our greatest treasures.

Having to fuel my own desires and ambitions from an early age made me the self-starter that I am and I am thankful for this. While I once begrudged the fact that I did not have a fairy tale childhood, I now find that having to find my own way and having to be my own parent and life coach was actually a good thing.

My early teen years were a very pivotal time for me as I found myself filling my lone time with more useful pursuits, rather than filling them with feelings of emptiness and loneliness as I did in my earlier youth. I spent time reading and writing, developing a relationship to music and simply gazing out the window, looking for meaning. I began the lifelong process of self-discovery during those quiet moments in my bedroom and my creativity was born.

We all choose our parents for various reasons. Understanding the reasons is a big part of our healing. I am clear on some things, but the jury is still out on the others. However, it is now a moot point now, since visiting hauntings and performing clearings are some of my favorite things to do. I find the field very exciting, though it is not my professional focus. My professional focus is helping people find a connection to their soul and purpose.

Heaven on Earth...

As I lay awake late at night, my radio alarm clock would make a clicking sound when the numbers 11:11 made an appearance. A chill would run through me each time and something inside of me knew it bore significance. Through the years, I have met others who experienced the same thing, one of whom was my youngest brother. Although we all felt it must have significance, we did not know what it was.

Around the same time period, which was in the early 70's, I was perusing my Bible and came across a phrase that said that one day, Heaven and Earth would be as one. Upon reading that statement, I paused and immediately felt that the appearance of the 11:11 had something to do with this, as though spirit was trying to communicate something with me. My next thought was that the merging of Heaven and Earth would occur in my lifetime. Although this rang true to me, I passed it off as a wild imagining. That was too big of a thought for someone like little old me to conjure up.

I mention these things because I feel we should trust those things that come to us in moments of inner clarity. These are things that are coming from the unmanifested.

It would be more than 20 years later that these realizations would begin to make sense to me. With the proliferation of the spiritual new age, others have risen up and proclaimed that this is the time when the Earth will be restored to its natural state, which is Heaven on Earth. There are also millions of results on the Internet when one searches 11:11. Those moments I had when younger were now being validated.

I was actually in a state of meditation at many times, without realizing it. I was tuned into the cosmos, making discoveries that would come to light much later in my life. Nonetheless, spirit continued trying to communicate with me even though I was not yet ready to listen. The connection to my soul now became a much higher priority than it ever was.

In retrospect, I have noted that these openings began to occur in a group during a time when my lower self was once again completely exhausted – leaving an opening for my spirit to resurface. I consulted spirit medium, Anne

Marie of Milwaukee in an effort to find some meaning in the events that were unfolding and all she could say to me at that time was that it was my life purpose to be a spirit medium and that the light of God shined through me. She didn't have much more to say - the rest was up to me to discover. Nobody had ever said anything like this to me and it struck a nerve. The pump was primed and my life began to move in a different direction, creating the opening for more synchronicity and etheric help.

Eventually I came to understand that my Love of Spirit and my open and willing heart actually emitted a light, which is a healing energy. Before I understood this, I was easily taken advantage of and used by others. It was time that I learned what God's plan was for this energy. Events began to pull things together for me an accelerated as time went on.

While working at a client's home where I was installing wallpaper, the homeowner began asking me probing questions about my philosophy of life. After a long list of questions, she squarely asked me, "Where is Heaven?" I turned around without answering and looked at her and she said, "It is right here." We ended up talking for hours and eventually discovered that she also frequently saw 11:11 on the clock and knew it had spiritual significance.

We parted that day committed to determining what the meaning of 11:11 was and indeed we were introduced to a book called 11:11, Inside the Doorway by Solara. We were not alone. There was a clear connection in the unmanifested and we all knew it had heavenly connotations.

My soul had been trying to communicate with me all my life and I was finally ready to listen. The soul gives us nudges and waits patiently for us to give it permission to forge on.

My psychic channels having been opened wide as a result of these events. I began to become more open to my sensitivity to energies again, and began to know who was calling when the phone rang and so on. Right around the same time, I was incurring a gradual emotional breakdown as repeated mentions of horrific crimes in metro Milwaukee threatened my vision of humanity and the safety of my young children.

I always had a tendency to be empathetic largely because I see all of humanity as one being. I feel the pain of others and take things very personally. Also, many people that I knew had been passing away at an unnatural pace and one Friday afternoon, I broke down and began to cry because it was my last resort to relieve the tension and frustration I was feeling.

I rifled through the Bible and prayed to Jesus, trying to find an answer and could not. I so believed in the goodness of God and the goodness of mankind, yet I was being repeatedly disappointed and horrified by what I was experiencing.

I know that many others have felt the same way. How could a good God let bad things happen? A good man that I had just met and knew for a brief period of time had just passed away – a loving husband and father of an adorable baby boy. I desperately needed to know why mean people survive to perpetrate such dastardly deeds

About the Author 119

while good people perish? Little did I know that my understanding of spirituality was about to take a huge leap.

At the time, I did not know why, but the crying was feeling very warming and good as I went deeper into my being. Actually, tears are cleansing and they cause a release of feel good chemicals. I felt enveloped by Love and began to realize many things that had gone unanswered for me in my life. I did not try to stop the tears because they felt good and decided to see where they would lead me. With tear filled eyes, I stood in line at the grocery store and saw a beautiful face on the front of a paperback book: A Return to Love by Marianne Williamson. I still remember the moment I discovered it and it looked like a mirage at first.

I knew this book was for me and as I read it, the me that I had buried and left behind so many years ago began to come back to life. I subsequently obtained my copy of *A Course In Miracles,* which was the book that motivated Williamson to write *A Return to Love.*

Up until this point, I had lost track of much of who I was when I was younger and these two books played such a large role in helping me return to my true self. As a young adult, I finally realized the Love had been benched for me because I did not know what to do with it. I knew that the answers that I needed were in that text and the day I finally opened up to the first page was the first day of the rest of my life. The introduction reads:

"This is a course in miracles. It is a required course. Only the time you take it is voluntary. Free will does not mean that you can establish the curriculum. It means only that you can elect what you want to take at a given time. The course does not aim at teaching the meaning of love, for that is beyond what can be taught. It does aim, however, at removing the blocks to the awareness of love's presence, which is your natural inheritance. The opposite of love is fear, but what is all encompassing can have no opposite.

The teachings in this book took me to the holiest of holy places inside of me and it was as though I had stepped into a transformation tank or a time tunnel and something so all encompassing and ancient took over my being and my full spiritual vision was installed. I had new software! Everything now had new meaning and everything looked different. I could see the energies beneath that which we see with our shallow ego vision. I felt as though I was really and truly myself in this place. This was the eternal me. I loved this place and I never let go of it again.

My intuitive abilities and inner peace had reached a level that I had never yet experienced in this life and while it was surreal, it also felt so right and so natural. Answers now came quickly and I was like a child with a new toy. I realized that every day presented me with new horizons and that I was being led back to my fully realized self: step-by-step, day-by-day. I could feel the stream of energy go out before me and lead me to the next destination with new insights every day.

This is a good example of how asking or prayer will lead us and guide us and also how the creative works of another human being can serve as such a life saver. I have heard people say that it is not possible for one human to learn from another, but that just depends on whether or not we are teachable. We are all so integral and everybody has a book to write - once they know their story.

The teachings and restoration that I underwent during my acceleration were divinely guided and of course, the proof is in the pudding. In the early nineties, I had my aura picture taken during a bookstore spirit fair, by a woman who owned a Kirlian camera. This is a camera that picks up the color or vibration of the energy of the subject it is focused on. The camera produced a Polaroid picture as well as a computer printout. As the printout was coming out of her computer, she was exclaiming, "Oh my God, I have never seen this before. Your aura is all ultraviolet light!" This means that, at least at that moment, everything that I was, both physical and spiritual was in the state of pure consciousness. In this state, we are in full communication with the divine. Christ Consciousness produces this state of clarity and pure bliss.

It is important to mention this because, having experienced the freedom of this level of consciousness, I am able to help others achieve it as well. Just recently in 2014, I had another aura picture taken and this camera showed me as having an all white aura. I have maintained this disposition for two decades, although admittedly, I have had my days. Depending on the equipment used and the sensitivity thereof, white and ultra violet would be closely related if not the same. It is possible to stay in this state, yet is can be challenging when surrounded by human drama.

This state gives me a clear perspective and I am able to see the heart of individuals and am able to ask the masters questions and hear the answers because I am vibrating high enough to be tuned into them.

As time went on, the spirits that once haunted me as a child were no longer scary as I learned that I can set boundaries for my sensitivity. I began doing readings for other people and learned about the Akashic records, which is the band of consciousness that holds all of the historical information of the physical unfolding of humanity and the planet. It is accessed through our heart chakras and the history is imprinted therein. Do you realize that you are carrying around your very own copy of your soul history in the electromagnetic data of your chakras?

The information I received via these channels was astonishing, clear and accurate – cutting to the quick and allowing my clients to get clarity on things that they were previously confused by. I also received information regarding the mind-body connection to their illnesses and how their history related to physical symptoms. The assistance of the other side or the invisible is there to serve us and make life easier. My earlier experiences were simply demonstrations of the power and connectedness of the subtle realms.

During the years that I was doing many readings, I discovered that everybody goes through the same process that I had been going through, simply at a different pace and often without the knowledge that I had. This is what *A Course in Miracles* refers to as the curriculum. We get stuck in one place and feel like we are going in circles unless we know how to resolve the karma that is holding us back.

When we are able to review the evolution of an individual soul and tap into its goals and history, we can then make the necessary changes and heal what needs to be healed in a very personalized, specific way. There are laws of metaphysics operating at all times, yet most people do not know how to tap into them. Trained intuitives will turn this world around in a way that psychiatry may never do.

Working to find peace amidst the turmoil has been a constant process. I have never opted to use alcohol or drugs to cope. Once I asked my guides when this turbulence around me would end, and the answer I heard was, "When you no longer see it as difficulty." I came to realize that the discordant energies around me forced me inward with a focus that grew in a slow but positive manner until I the awareness of my spirit became brighter and stronger than the outer forces.

Peeling back the layers of my ego was a long process, and building my spirit has been the most rewarding thing I have ever done. There is not a retirement plan, job title or fancy car that can replace feeling good inside and outside.

I want to share everything I have learned because I believe in the human being's ability to overcome and achieve. I believe in personal responsibility and perseverance and further resolve that if enough people embrace their path, we will find our way out of the seeming financial crisis and many other problems that we are experiencing as a group.

Journaling Space

About the Author 125

About the Author 127

About the Author

About the Author 131

About the Author 135

About the Author